D0153878

POLICY AND PRACTICE IN HEALTH AND SOCIAL CARE
NUMBER TWENTY-SIX

Human Rights and Social Care

Putting rights into practice

POLICY AND PRACTICE IN HEALTH AND SOCIAL CARE

1: Jacqueline Atkinson, *Private and Public Protection: Civil Mental Health Legislation* (2006) – Out of Print

2: Charlotte Pearson (ed.), *Direct Payments and Personalisation of Care* (2006) – Out of Print

3: Joyce Cavaye, *Hidden Carers* (2006) – Out of Print

4: Mo McPhail (ed.), *Service User and Carer Involvement: Beyond Good Intentions* (2007) – Out of Print

5: Anne Stafford, *Safeguarding and Protecting Children and Young People* (2008) – Out of Print

6: Alison Petch, *Health and Social Care: Establishing a Joint Future?* (2007) – Out of Print

7: Gillian MacIntyre, *Learning Disability and Social Inclusion* (2008) – Out of Print

8: Ailsa Cook, *Dementia and Well-Being: Possibilities and Challenges* (2008) – Out of Print

9: Michele Burman and Jenny Johnstone (eds.), *Youth Justice* (2009) – Out of Print

10: Rebecca L. Jones and Richard Ward (eds.), *LGBT Issues: Looking Beyond Categories* (2009) – Out of Print

11: Jacqueline H. Watts, *Death, Dying and Bereavement: Issues for Practice* (2009)

12: Richard Hammersley, *Drugs* (2012)

13: Ailsa Stewart, *Supporting Vulnerable Adults: Citizenship, Capacity, Choice* (2012)

14: Emma Miller, *Individual Outcomes: Getting Back to What Matters* (2011)

15: Ken Barrie, *Alcohol* (2012)

16: Gary Clapton and Pauline Hoggan, *Adoption & Fostering in Scotland* (2012)

17: Graham Connelly and Ian Milligan, *Residential Child Care: Between Home and Family* (2012)

18: Gary Clapton, *Social Work with Fathers: Positive Practice* (2013)

19: Charlotte Pearson, Julie Ridley and Susan Hunter, *Self-Directed Support* (2014)

20: Fiona Garven, Jennifer McLean and Lisa Pattoni, *Asset-Based Approaches: Their rise, role and reality* (2016)

21: Philomena de Lima, *International Migration* (2017)

22: Oona Brooks-Hay, Michele Burman and Clare McFeely, *Domestic Abuse* (forthcoming 2018)

23: Nigel Sprigings, *Housing and Housing Management: Balancing the two key contracts* (2017)

24: Charlotte L. Clarke *et al.* (eds), *Risk and Resilience: Global learning across the age span* (2017)

25: Kate Norman, *Socialising Transgender: Support in transition* (2017)

26: Sam Smith, *Human Rights and Social Care: Putting rights into practice* (forthcoming 2018)

27: Fiona Cuthill, *Homelessness, Social Exclusion and Health: Global perspectives, local solutions* (forthcoming 2018)

See www.dunedinacademicpress.co.uk for details of all our publications

POLICY AND PRACTICE IN HEALTH AND SOCIAL CARE
SERIES EDITORS
CHARLOTTE L. CLARKE AND CHARLOTTE PEARSON

Human Rights and Social Care
Putting rights into practice

Sam Smith
CEO, C-Change Scotland, Glasgow (www.c-change.org.uk)

DUNEDIN

EDINBURGH ◆ LONDON

First published in 2018 by Dunedin Academic Press Ltd.
Head Office: Hudson House, 8 Albany Street, Edinburgh EH1 3QB
London Office: 352 Cromwell Tower, Barbican, London EC2Y 8NB

ISBNs:
9781780460673 (Paperback)
9781780465906 (ePub)
9781780465913 (Kindle)

British Library Cataloguing in Publication Data
A catalogue record for this book is available from the British Library

Typeset by Makar Publishing Production, Edinburgh
Printed in Great Britain by CPI Antony Rowe

'It is in each other's shadows that we flourish.'

Mary Robinson, speaking at the launch of the
Scottish Human Rights Commission in July 2008.

CONTENTS

	Acknowledgements	ix
	Glossary of Abbreviations	xi
	Introduction	xiii
Chapter 1	Towards Human Rights and Social Care	1
Chapter 2	The Rights of the Child	25
	with Juliet Harris	
Chapter 3	The Rights of Women	48
Chapter 4	The Rights of Disabled People	66
Chapter 5	The Rights of Older Persons	99
Chapter 6	Conclusion: The Way Forward	117
Appendix 1	European Convention on Human Rights	121
Appendix 2	UK Human Rights Commitments	128
	References	129
	Index	140

ACKNOWLEDGEMENTS

Thank you to my family, friends and colleagues for their unwavering support while I wrote this book. A special thanks to Stanley who was by my side the whole time.

GLOSSARY OF ABBREVIATIONS

ASP	Adult Support and Protection (Scotland) Act 2007
AWI	Adults With Incapacity (Scotland) Act 2000
BME	black and minority ethnic
CEDAW	Convention on the Elimination of All Forms of Discrimination against Women
CESCR	Committee on Economic, Social and Cultural Rights
COSLA	Coalition of Scottish Local Authorities
CRC	Committee on the Rights of the Child
CRPD	Convention on the Rights of Persons with Disabilities
DOLS	Deprivation of Liberty Safeguards
ECHR	European Convention on Human Rights
ECtHR	European Court of Human Rights
EHRC	Equality and Human Rights Commission
FRA	European Union Agency for Fundamental Rights
HRA	Human Rights Act 1998
HRBA	Human Rights Based Approach
HRC	Human Rights Committee
ICCPR	International Covenant on Civil and Political Rights
ICESCR	International Covenant on Economic, Social and Cultural Rights
LGB	lesbian, gay or bisexual
LGBT	lesbian, gay, bisexual and transgender
MCA	Mental Capacity Act 2005
MHA	Mental Health (Care and Treatment) (Scotland) Act 2003
MWC	Mental Welfare Commission for Scotland
NGO	non-governmental organisations
NHRI	national human rights institutions
NRS	National Records of Scotland
ONS	Office for National Statistics
PANEL	Participation; Accountability; Non-Discrimination and Equality; Empowerment; and Legality

PCT	Primary Care Trust
SA	Scotland Act 1998
SCQF	Scottish Credit and Qualifications Framework
SDS	Self-Directed Support
SHRC	Scottish Human Rights Commission
SNAP	Scottish National Action Plan
UDHR	Universal Declaration of Human Rights
UK	United Kingdom
UN	United Nations
UNCRC	UN Convention on the Rights of the Child

INTRODUCTION

> Where, after all, do universal human rights begin? In small places, close to home – so close and so small that they cannot be seen on any maps of the world. Yet they are the world of the individual person; the neighbourhood (s)he lives in; the school or college (s)he attends; the factory, farm, or office where (s)he works. Such are the places where every man, woman, and child seeks equal justice, equal opportunity, equal dignity without discrimination. Unless these rights have meaning there, they have little meaning anywhere. Without concerted citizen action to uphold them close to home, we shall look in vain for progress in the larger world (Eleanor Roosevelt).[1]

I have taken the liberty of slightly amending (in *italics*) this famous quote by Eleanor Roosevelt to address the gender-specific nature of the original statement. However, the sentiment prevails and provides the focus for this book, which aims to act as a counterbalance to the notion of human rights, and human rights law, as the preserve of lawyers, courtrooms and judges. This is not to say that the legal profession and the court of law are not important in the realisation of human rights. They are, and careful attention will be paid throughout this volume to particularly significant case law that has set precedent for the development of human rights jurisprudence. The focus of this book, however, is on the universality of human rights and the role of the citizen in manifesting and bringing these rights to life, in the living breathing reality of our day-to-day lives. Its aim is to contribute to a growing understanding of the power and potential of human rights in the many different roles citizens fulfil daily as family

---

1 Excerpt from a speech at the presentation of 'In Your Hands: A Guide for Community Action for the Tenth Anniversary of the Universal Declaration of Human Rights', Thursday, 27 March 1958, United Nations, New York. As head of the Human Rights Commission, Eleanor Roosevelt was instrumental in formulating the Universal Declaration of Human Rights, which she submitted to the UN General Assembly with these words: 'We stand today at the threshold of a great event both in the life of the United Nations and in the life of mankind. This declaration may well become the international Magna Carta for all men everywhere.'

members, as colleagues, as those in receipt of additional support and as professionals working in the field of social care. Human rights are, if understood, owned and exercised, a set of shared values and aspirations that form a common lexicon of oneness in our humanity, that transcends age, gender, race, religion, disability and sexual orientation. In that, they can be the source of great inspiration, power and solidarity.

CHAPTER 1

Towards Human Rights and Social Care

> That there are limitations to the law in human services is indisputable. That the rule of law is indispensable to a civilised society is equally indisputable. At best, the law ideally provides a mechanism by which justice can ultimately triumph over injustice, but that will never happen for vulnerable persons unless the common streams of rights and advocacy continue to flow. The law in and of itself does not protect people; people protect people, if necessary by shaping and invoking laws that express society's commitment to dignity and equality for all persons (Orville Endicott).[1]

Introduction

Human rights belong to us; by the very nature of our humanity they are ours to exercise and realise (EHRC, 2014a). Their universality means they are inclusive of all and, consequently, they have the potential to challenge social orders based on exclusion (de Feyter, 2011). Human rights are indivisible, in that those in positions of authority and power cannot pick and choose which rights to respect. A right is an entitlement that endures 'even when the right holder is not actually making a verbal claim' (Orend, 2002, p. 24). The very inalienability of human rights, the fact that they cannot be taken away from someone, should require all those involved in social care to know and understand the human rights framework within which they operate. Human rights are inabrogable, meaning that they cannot be given up voluntarily or traded for additional

---

1 Legal Counsel at Community Living Ontario, in Toronto, Canada . He wrote this statement in 2011 in the preface (Wolfensberger, 2013, p. 5).

privileges. Human rights impact on every aspect of our lives and can, if developed to their full potential, be a powerful driver for positive change in our homes, in our communities, our schools and our workplaces. Human rights provide an internationally accepted set of conditions by which we, as citizens, should live with dignity, be respected and afforded the opportunity to flourish.

Some threats to human dignity, such as poverty and violence, may originate, at least in part, beyond national borders. As human rights are now generally recognised as a matter of international concern, framing a claim in human rights terms creates the possibility of drawing on support from external forces (de Feyter, 2011). With the development of the Internet and social media, this support may come from allies around the world. Using the language of human rights potentially leverages change by providing an internationally recognised and agreed lexicon. Recognising the implications of international issues such as climate change, extremist violence and forced migration, there is a need to move from human rights declarations into 'times of implementation' (Miller, 2016, p. 2).

International human rights law is a broad and complex arena. This book will focus on specific UN Conventions relating to children, women and disabled people and more specifically the European Convention on Human Rights (ECHR), the regional human rights Convention with relevant application to the UK. The discussion of human rights and social care within this work is rooted in the philosophical context of citizenship and social justice.

The development of international human rights

The conceptual precursor to modern human rights can be traced back to ancient civilisations (Ishay, 2004). The Magna Carta (1215)[2] is also cited as the first legal recognition of individual rights (Freeman, 2002). A line is often drawn between the natural law theorists of the Enlightenment, such as Thomas Hobbes and John Locke, and the development of human rights in the mid-twentieth century (Ife, 2012; Freeman, 2002).

The modern system of human rights can be traced back to the devas-

---

2 Magna Carta, meaning 'The Great Charter', was originally issued by King John of England (r.1199–1216). It established for the first time the principle that everybody, including the king, was subject to the law. Magna Carta remains a cornerstone of the British constitution. Available from URL: www.bl.uk/magna-carta/articles (accessed 15 February 2018).

tating global events of the first half of the twentieth century. Two world wars, the Great Depression and the Holocaust led the world to restate the common values of humanity. The Universal Declaration of Human Rights (UDHR),[3] adopted by the UN General Assembly in 1948, defined human rights as the fundamental freedoms of thought, opinion, expression and belief (Skegg, 2005). The declaration was intended to create a benchmark of standards for people of all nations to enjoy regardless of nationality, race, ethnicity, culture, age or gender (Robson, 1997):

> Human rights are equal rights: one either is or is not a human being, and therefore has the same human rights as everyone else (or none at all). They are also inalienable rights: one cannot stop being human, no matter how badly one behaves or how barbarously one is treated. And they are universal rights, in the sense that today we consider all members of the species *Homo sapiens* 'human beings', and thus holders of human rights (Donnelly, 2003, p. 10).

The international community increasingly began to use the language of human rights to address issues of human dignity (de Feyter, 2011). The UDHR was and remains a beacon of hope, influencing a wide range of international and regional human rights treaties that developed subsequently. The evolution of the modern system of international human rights in the twentieth and twenty-first centuries is often described as taking place in three phases or generations. This simplistic and linear characterisation should not obscure the overlapping indivisible nature of human rights.

The UDHR, together with the International Covenant on Civil and Political Rights (ICCPR) and its two Optional Protocols,[4] and the International Covenant on Economic, Social and Cultural Rights

---

3 Universal Declaration of Human Rights (UDHR), GA Res. 217A (III), UN Doc. A/810 at 71 (1948).

4 Optional Protocols to human rights treaties are treaties in their own right, and are open to signature, accession or ratification by countries who are party to the main treaty. The First Optional Protocol to the ICCPR is an international treaty establishing an individual complaint mechanism for the ICCPR. It was adopted by the UN General Assembly on 16 December 1966, and entered into force on 23 March 1976. Available from URL: www. ohchr.org/EN/ProfessionalInterest/Pages/OPCCPR1.aspx (accessed 12 March 2018). The Second Optional aimed to bring about the abolition of the death penalty. It was adopted and proclaimed by General Assembly resolution 44/128 of 15 December 1989. Available from URL: www.ohchr.org/EN/ProfessionalInterest/Pages/2ndOPCCPR.aspx (accessed 12 March 2018).

(ICESCR) form what is commonly called the International Bill of Rights. UDHR privileged civil and political rights such as the right to a fair trial and the right to vote and provided less of a focus on economic, social and cultural rights. The postwar, cold-war struggle between the competing ideologies of democracy and communism may have influenced the prioritisation of certain rights. There exists legitimate criticism that early definitions of human rights potentially overvalued Western ideals of individualism and were less relevant to the rest of the world's developing needs (Bauer, 1999). First-generation rights are largely negative ones, in that states are required to refrain from certain actions. The ICCPR[5] has found articulation in the ECHR.

Second-generation rights outlined in the ICESCR[6] include areas such as the right to housing, adequate food and healthcare. They are described as positive rights as they require the State to undertake positive action to fulfil the international rights obligations. Third-generation rights are those at a collective level for communities, populations, societies or nations: for example, the right to breathe unpolluted air; the right to economic development (Williams, 2004). Common to the preamble of the Covenants is the phrase 'human rights derive from the inherent dignity of the human person'. The purpose of human rights is not only to recognise the inherent dignity of humankind but also to achieve human dignity. Human rights treaties create legal obligations with the aim of safeguarding the dignity of all human persons (de Feyter, 2011, p. 12). Human rights treaties, processes and obligations have a greater purpose than the protection of the individual claimant (important as that is); they have a wider local, national and international social impact.

The Vienna Convention on the Law of Treaties was agreed in 1969 and came into force in 1980; it codified rules relating to international agreements. It is generally accepted that international law will apply to a State regardless of its domestic law. Article 27 of the Vienna Convention provides that a State cannot plead conflict with its own domestic law as an excuse for contravention of international obligations (Finch and McGroarty, 2014).

---

5 International Covenant on Civil and Political Rights, New York, 16 December 1966, in force 23 March 1976, GA Res. 2200A (XXI), UN Doc. A/6316 (1966); 999 UNTS 171; 6 ILM 368.

6 International Covenant on Economic, Social and Cultural Rights, New York, 16 December 1966, in force 3 January 1976, GA Res.2200A (XXI), UN Doc. A/6316 (1966); 993 UNTS 3; 6 ILM 368 (1967).

At the start of the new millennium, world heads of State and governments resolved 'to strive for full protection and promotion in all our countries of civil, political, economic, social and cultural rights for all'.[7]

There are several stages in the procedure for States to undertake when entering into international human rights agreements. Willing member States indicate their agreement to be bound by the obligations in the treaty or Convention through a process of ratification. Member States are then bound by international law. Several actions can be taken to limit the scope of a treaty. Prior to ratification, States can enter reservations, which have the effect of limiting the extent to which they will be bound by specific provisions. In addition, some international human rights agreements provide the facility for States to derogate from certain obligations in given circumstances. For example, Article 15 of the ECHR allows for derogation from some obligations given certain circumstances such as war or public emergencies.

Whether ratification automatically leads to incorporation into the domestic law of a signatory State depends upon the constitution of the State. Some countries such as Germany and France have a 'monist' approach, which means that international law takes precedence over domestic law. In such countries, ratification leads to the agreement being 'self-executing'. In countries where the constitution is based on a 'dualist approach', such as the United Kingdom (UK), international agreements are not incorporated into domestic law until legislation is passed which explicitly incorporates them, such as is the case with the Human Rights Act 1998 (Carver, 2010).

European Convention on Human Rights (ECHR)

The ECHR was signed in Rome in 1950 and came into force in 1953. It was the first comprehensive treaty in the field of human rights and was the first to introduce an international complaints procedure and international court for the determination of human rights matters. The ECHR is made up of fifty-nine Articles and has, over time, been amended and updated through the addition of a series of Protocols.

Article 1 of the Convention outlines the obligation to respect human

---

7   United Nations Millennium Declaration, GA Res. 55/2, UN Doc. A/Res/55/2 (2000), paras 24–25 of 59 Articles and has, over time, been amended and updated through the addition of a series of Protocols.

rights stating: 'The High Contracting Parties shall secure to everyone within their jurisdiction the rights and freedoms defined in Section (I) of this Convention.' Section I outlines the rights and freedoms in Articles 2–18. Section (II) outlines Articles specific to the European Court of Human Rights, and Section (III) considers miscellaneous provisions. See Appendix 1 for details of the main ECHR Articles relevant to the subject matter of this book.[8]

The ECHR allows for both individual petition (Article 34) and inter-state complaints (Article 33). The latter was more common in the early years of the European Court of Human Rights (ECtHR) and, while not used frequently, is still important. Individual petitions, which can be brought by individuals, legal persons (such as corporations), groups of individuals or non-governmental organisations, have grown significantly in number. To undertake an individual petition, domestic remedy requires to have been exhausted and the petition needs to be submitted within six months of the final decision in the domestic forum. The matter must also not concern an issue which is substantially the same as one that has already been examined by the ECtHR (Article 35).

The ECHR operates three levels of rights: absolute rights, procedural rights and qualified rights. Absolute rights cannot be derogated from under any circumstance; this would include Article 2 (right to life) and Article 3 (prohibition of torture).[9] Procedural rights would include Article 6 (the right to a fair trial). Qualified rights include the right to respect for private and family life, home and correspondence (Article 8, ECHR). Article 8 is particularly relevant to social care policy and practice. As with any qualified right, any limitation should have a basis in the law, pursue a legitimate aim or goal and be proportionate. i.e. the least restrictive necessary to achieve the legitimate aim.

---

8 The full text of the European Convention on Human Rights can be found at www.echr.coe. int/Pages/home.aspx?p=basictexts&c (accessed 12 March 2018).

9 The European Convention on Human Rights affords to the governments of the States parties, in exceptional circumstances, the possibility of derogating, in a temporary, limited and supervised manner, from their obligation to secure certain rights and freedoms under the Convention. The use of that provision is governed by the following procedural and substantive conditions. There is no facility to derogate from Article 2 [right to life], except in respect of deaths resulting from lawful acts of war, or from Articles 3 [prohibition of torture and inhuman or degrading treatment or punishment], 4 (para 1) [prohibition of slavery and servitude] and 7 [no punishment without law] shall be made under this provision. Available from URL: www.echr.coe.int/Documents/FS_Derogation_ENG.pdf (accessed 16 February 2018).

The legal discipline of human rights consists of interpreting abstract rules to determine their concrete meaning in a particular context, leading to an assessment of whether a local incident involved a violation or not (de Feyter, 2011, p. 14). The key difference between many international human rights conventions and the ECHR is that it has an infrastructure for application and enforcement. State parties enjoy a margin of appreciation as to how they apply and implement the Convention, depending upon the circumstances of the case and the rights and freedoms engaged.[10] This reflects that the Convention system is subsidiary to the safeguarding of human rights at national level and that national authorities are, in principle, better placed than an international court to evaluate local needs and conditions (Alston and Goodman, 2012).

European Court of Human Rights (ECtHR)

The ECtHR came into being in 1959. It sits in Strasbourg and is made up of judges nominated by each of the signatory States to the ECHR. Judges are elected by the Parliamentary Assembly of the Council of Europe for a term of six years. They sit as individuals and not as representatives of their State. The Court does not base its judgements on legal precedent when deciding cases before it. Its role is not to operate as an appeal court for the decisions of national tribunals but rather to ensure that the standards of the Convention and Protocols are observed by the administrations of the State parties (Brownlie and Goodwin-Gill, 2010). The ECtHR adopted the doctrine of the ECHR as a 'living instrument which [...] must be interpreted in light of present-day conditions'.[11] Also, that the Convention should be interpreted in a manner which ensures rights are not theoretical or illusory, but practical and effective.[12]

---

10 The margin of appreciation is a doctrine that the European Court of Human Rights has developed when considering whether a member state has breached the Convention. It affords a member state a degree of discretion, subject to Strasbourg supervision, when taking legislative, administrative or judicial action in the area of a Convention right. The doctrine allows the Court to consider the fact that the Convention will be interpreted differently in different member states, given their divergent legal and cultural traditions. The margin of appreciation gives the Court the necessary flexibility to balance the sovereignty of member states with their obligations under the Convention. Available from URL: www.opensocietyfoundations.org/sites/default/files/echr-reform-margin-of-appreciation.pdf (accessed 12 March 2018).

11 European Court of Human Rights, *Tyrer v. UK*, Judgement of 23 April 1978, Series A, No. 26 (1978), para 31.

12 See European Court of Human Rights, *Artico v. Italy*, Judgement of 13 May 1980, [1980] ECHR Series A, No. 37, para 33.

Human rights in the UK

In the UK, while the sovereign occupies the position as head of State, the ability to make and pass laws resides with an elected Parliament; this arrangement is characterised as a constitutional monarchy. The UK does not have a written constitution, and many of its civil and political protections have evolved over time 'as a result of legislation and common law development, not any bill of rights' (Heydon, 2014, p. 393). Common law was considered to protect liberties by providing remedies rather than enforcing rights: 'there is in the English constitution an absence of those declarations or definitions of rights so dear to foreign constitutionalists' (Dicey, 1959, p. 144). This rather benign view of historical human rights protections is not uncontested in the literature. Some have suggested that not all rights were protected in this arrangement: 'there was harassment and ill treatment of dissenters and outsiders and petty abuse of power in prisons, police cells, schools and mental institutions, often condoned low in the hierarchy' (Simpson, 2004, p. 51). It has been noted that Britain remains 'one of the few advanced democracies to rely so heavily upon the legislature to defend human rights' (Bogdanor, 2009, p. 55).

The right to individual petition from the UK to Strasbourg came into force in 1966, and the ECHR entered into the constitutional systems of the UK in 1998 with the introduction of the Human Rights Act. Up to that point, successive governments had refused to incorporate the ECHR on the basis that it was perceived unnecessary and considered to be an interference with the sovereignty of Westminster. This remains a highly contested area of debate. Despite these reservations, at the end of the twentieth century two significant Acts of Parliament – the Human Rights Act 1998 (HRA) and the Scotland Act 1998 (SA) – received the Royal Assent in November 1998 (Miller, 2000), and it is to an analysis of the implications of this legislation we now turn.

Human Rights Act 1998 (HRA)

The HRA came into force in 2000 and sought to enable domestic courts to apply the ECHR, subject to respect for parliamentary sovereignty. The aim was to provide domestic remedy, thereby obviating the need for application to the Strasbourg institutions (Reed and Murdoch, 2001, p. vi). In brief, the HRA contains three main elements: firstly, ministers are now required to certify whether new legislation complies with the European Convention; secondly, Courts are obliged to interpret all legislation so that it is compatible with the Convention; and thirdly, in such circumstances that the legislation cannot be construed to be made compatible with Convention rights, then the Courts may issue a declaration of incompatibility (Bogdanor, 2009). The HRA affords the ECHR a unique position in the UK legal and constitutional system, with a status higher than an 'ordinary' Act of the Westminster Parliament while falling short of being constitutionally guaranteed within the UK (Reed and Murdoch, 2001, p. 8). The HRA does not 'incorporate' the ECHR but is 'an Act to give further effect to rights and freedoms under the ECHR' (Reed and Murdoch, 2001, p. 10). The HRA introduced, for the first time into the legal system of the UK, a definitive framework in which the fundamental civil and political rights of the individual are balanced with the public interest. Some argue that, with the enactment of HRA, judicial powers to protect human rights have been substantially increased because of the interpretative function (Kavanagh, 2004, p. 275). Further, that the HRA makes the ECHR, in effect, part of the fundamental law of the land. Despite this assertion, rights are clearly still dependent upon the discretion of Parliament (Miller, 2016, p. 64).

Scotland Act 1998 (SA)

Until comparatively recently, the concept of human rights did not form a recognised part of the Scottish legal system (Reed and Murdoch, 2008, p. 1). This is not to suggest that human rights were not protected, merely that they lacked a clearly defined and protected constitutional status. Before embarking upon an analysis of the SA, it is worth reflecting briefly upon the distinctly Scottish cultural and legal characteristics that inform the approach to human rights and that are clearly distinguishable from the English approach.

It has been argued that there exists an historic and distinctively Scottish perspective on rights which, unlike the English or Anglo-American perspective, takes the position that an individual's rights are a 'right to personality' (Reed and Murdoch, 2001, p. 1). It is suggested that the SA is broadly based on the Scottish Constitutional Convention's blueprint, Scotland's Parliament, Scotland's Right, which among other things proposed a Charter of Rights for Scotland (Miller, 2000, p. 16).

At the inaugural meeting in March 1989, a Claim of Right was adopted – the third in Scotland's history. The stated purpose was 'to root the Convention solidly in an historic Scottish Constitutional principle that power is limited, should be dispersed and is derived from the people' (Miller, 2000, p. 15).

The introduction of the HRA and the SA has been described as 'the most profound constitutional and legal change in Scotland for the past three centuries' (Miller, 2000, p. 3). The HRA is mentioned in the SA and as such is embedded in the devolution settlement. The Scottish Parliament may not pass laws which are incompatible with the rights in the HRA.[13] It is also prevented from making law or any other activity which would be incompatible with the HRA.[14]

This means that any act of the Scottish Government which is incompatible with the ECHR would have no legal effect, and that any legislation passed which was outside legislative competence is not law.[15] What this means in operation is that, although Scottish Courts can only make declarations of incompatibility in respect of acts of the UK government, they can, in fact, invalidate Acts of the Scottish Parliament if they are judged to be incompatible with the ECHR.[16] Scottish Courts were slow at first to make use of the ECHR[17]. In 1997, Lord Hope made a seminal statement on the status of the ECHR in Scots Law,[18] which had a knock-on effect on informing judgements in Scotland. Given the different constitutional character, the domestication of European Convention rights has a more immediate and significant impact in Scotland than in the rest of the UK: 'a consequence of the Scotland Act is that human rights enjoy a more enhanced status in Scotland than the rest of the UK' (Miller, 2000, p. 11).

---

13 Scotland Act 1998, s.29(2)(d).

14 Scotland Act 1998, s.57(2).

15 Section 57(2) and Section 29(1) of the Scotland Act 1998.

16 Schedule 6 of the Scotland Act 1998; Section 29(2)(d) of the Scotland Act 1998.

17 In the 1980 case of *Surjit Kaur v. Lord Advocate* 1980 SC 319, Lord Ross expressed the view that a Scottish Court was not entitled to have regard to the ECHR, either as an aid to construction or otherwise, unless and until its provisions were given statutory effect. This contrasted with the approach adopted by England and Wales, including by Scottish judges sitting in the House of Lords.

18 See *T, Petitioner* [1997] SLT 724 at 734 in which Lord Hope concluded: '... the courts in Scotland should apply the same presumption [...] namely that, when legislation is found to be ambiguous in the sense that it is capable of a meaning which either confirms to or conflicts with the Convention, Parliament is to be presumed to have legislated in conformity with the Convention, not in conflict with it.

Sovereignty

The recent high-profile debates regarding human rights and the repeal of the HRA have tended to focus on the issue of the perceived 'threat' to parliamentary sovereignty. While this may provide emotive headlines, it fails to take account of the fact that the HRA was drafted in such a way as to protect that fundamental constitutional tenet. The Courts cannot strike down laws of the Westminster Parliament found to be incompatible with Convention rights; rather they may issue a 'declaration of incompatibility'.[19] One of the most high-profile examples of this measure has been in relation to the issue of prisoner voting rights.[20]

The English and Scottish traditions relating to parliamentary sovereignty highlight a key point of divergence. Parliamentary sovereignty, the absence of legal limits on the power of Parliament, may be regarded as the fundamental rule of the British constitution. It is a legal or constitutional principle which, it is argued, gives effect to the political principle of popular sovereignty (Ewing, 1999, p. 99). This is not a tradition shared with Scotland, as stated by Lord President Cooper in the case of *McCormick v. Lord Advocate* 1953 SC 396: 'The principle of unlimited sovereignty of Parliament is a distinctively English principle which has no counterpart in Scottish constitutional law'.[21]

With the introduction of the SA, the limits of the Scottish Parliament are set out in statute. The task of ensuring that the devolved institution remains within the limits of the powers granted to it is one for the Courts: 'What has been created by the Devolution Statute then is a democratic institution, whose acts are, however, subject to control by the judiciary' (Reed and Murdoch, 2001, p. 33). As clearly stated by Lord President Rodger:

> [T]he Scottish Parliament [i]s a body which, however important its role, has been created by statute and derives its powers from statute ... In principle, therefore, the Parliament like any other body set up by law is subject to the law and to the courts which exist to uphold that law.[22]

---

19 Section 4, Human Rights Act 1998.

20 Wagner, A. (2011) 'Prisoner votes and the democratic deficit' (online), UK Human Rights Blog. Available from URL: https://ukhumanrightsblog.com/2011/09/20/prisoner-votes-and-the-democratic-deficit (accessed 16 February 2018).

21 *McCormick v. Lord Advocate* 1953 SC 396 in Miller, 2000, p. 16.

22 In *Whaley v. Lord Watson of Invergowrie*, 2000 S.L.T 475, (IH) per Lord President Rodger

The Scottish Parliament in keeping with its historical tradition has limited sovereignty. There has been ongoing debate about the level of divergence between the English and Scottish 'traditions' in relation to parliamentary sovereignty, particularly as applied by the courts. This is a rich seam for further debate and deliberation, which, unfortunately, is beyond the scope of this book.

International human rights commitments

The UK has made a wide range of international legal commitments to respect, protect and fulfil human rights by ratifying a range of UN Conventions. It has been slow to incorporate (bring into domestic law) these treaties (see Appendix 2: UK Human Rights Commitments). Only one international human rights treaty has such standing – the ECHR – which mainly protects civil and political rights.

Scotland: The national context

The purpose of the Scottish government is to focus government and public services on creating a more successful country. In doing so, it creates a vision for Scotland with broad measures of national well-being covering a range of economic, health, social and environmental indicators and targets. These were most recently articulated in the *National Performance Framework* (Scottish Government, 2016b), which describes what the government wants to achieve over the next ten years and provides a structure for delivery.

The Scottish government works with local government and provides funding and the framework for accountability and performance. Scotland's thirty-two local authorities are responsible for providing a range of public services. These include education, social care, roads and transport, economic development, housing and planning, environmental protection, waste management and cultural and leisure services. Local authorities have a range of powers and duties:

- mandatory duties – such as providing schooling for 5–16 year olds and social work services;
- permissive powers – such as economic development and recreation services;
- regulatory powers – such as trading standards, environmental health and licensing for taxis and public houses.[23]

---

at 481B in Reed and Murdoch, 2001, p. 33.

23 Available from URL: www.gov.scot/Topics/Government/local-government/localg (accessed 16 February 2018).

These duties and powers arise from a range of legislation such as the Social Care (Self-Directed Support) (Scotland) Act 2013 (designed to enable greater choice and control for people using social care services) and the Public Bodies (Joint Working) (Scotland) Act 2014 (which places a requirement on NHS Boards and local authorities to work together to deliver integrated health and social care services through Health and Social Care Partnerships). Both pieces of legislation were introduced following the report by the Christie Commission (Christie Commission, 2011).

Councils in Scotland operate independently of central government and are accountable to their electorates for the provision of services. While it could be argued that this enables greater democratic participation and accountability at the local level, it also poses challenges in ensuring consistent implementation of national strategy. This tension was highlighted in a progress report on the implementation of Self-Directed Support (SDS) (Audit Scotland, 2017), about which there will be more discussion later in this chapter.

National human rights institutions

The UK has established three national human rights institutions (NHRIs): The Northern Ireland Human Rights Commission, operationalised in 1999; the Equality and Human Rights Commission (EHRC), in 2007; and the Scottish Human Rights Commission (SHRC), in 2008. NHRIs are State bodies with a constitutional and/or legislative mandate to protect and promote human rights. Although funded by the State and part of the State apparatus, they operate and function independently from government. The general role of NHRIs is to address discrimination in all its forms, as well as to promote the protection of civil, political, economic, social and cultural rights. Core functions of NHRIs include complaint handling, human rights education and making recommendations on law reform.[24] When establishing a national human rights institution, a State is expected to comply with the UN principles relating to the status of national institutions, known as the Paris Principles.[25] NHRIs are the only public institutions that have the protection and promotion of human rights as their core mission (Kumar, 2006). A memorandum of

---

24 Available from URL: https://nhri.ohchr.org/EN/AboutUs/Pages/RolesTypesNHRIs. aspx (accessed 16 February 2018).

25 Paris Principles developed in Paris in 1991 and adopted by the UN General Assembly in 1993.

understanding has been agreed between the three UK commissions to foster cooperative working.

Scottish National Action Plan for Human Rights (SNAP)

The SHRC has consistently proposed that potential for human rights culture change is most enhanced where rights holders are empowered to know and claim their rights, where duty bearers can put those rights into practice and where there is sufficient accountability (SHRC, 2008). Discrimination, social exclusion and targeted victimisation and harassment have been identified as some of the principal causes of significant inequalities in Scotland (EHRC, 2010). The World Conference on Human Rights recommended that each State consider drawing up a national action plan identifying how it would improve the promotion and protection of human rights (UN General Assembly, 1993). In 2012, the SHRC published a document, *Getting It Right? Human Rights in Scotland*, which outlined the outcome of a three-year project considering the realisation of human rights in Scotland (SHRC, 2012). This document, a precursor to the Scottish National Action Plan (SNAP), noted that Scotland had made considerable progress in some areas, but this was not consistent across civil society. It noted that, while Scotland has developed a relatively strong legal and institutional framework for human rights and positive strategic and policy initiatives, the actual impact on the lived experience of the citizens of Scotland was inconsistent.

The SHRC identified three interconnected steps required for the realisation of human rights: structural steps, process steps and outcomes. Structural steps are described as the legal and institutional measures to protect human rights. This would include the ratification of international human rights treaties and their incorporation into domestic law. It also requires the development of regulatory bodies to ensure accountability and compliance of human rights in practice. Process steps include the development of strategies and policies that actively promote a human rights based approach (HRBA). These activities require the allocation of adequate resources to ensure implementation in practice. The third step relates to outcomes, the ability to determine the difference being made to the lives of people and communities who are affected. Significant progress has been made with steps one and two; there is more work necessary to establish real progress with step three.

In December 2013, the SHRC published Scotland's SNAP,[26] setting out key commitments aimed at improving human rights protection in Scotland (SHRC, 2013). The action plan was developed by a drafting group including the Scottish government, local authorities, the NHS and the Care Inspectorate. The purpose of SNAP is to coordinate action by public, private and voluntary bodies and individuals to achieve human dignity for all through the realisation of internationally recognised human rights. It is perceived to be the vehicle for embedding human rights into all areas of life in Scotland, helping to 'bridge the gap between people's legally recognised human rights and their everyday lives' (SHRC, 2013, p. 15).

Key areas of concern highlighted within SNAP include care, disability rights, health and criminal justice. Priority 4 states the intention to: 'enhance respect, protection and fulfilment of human rights to achieve high quality health and social care'. Commitments in the action plan include:

- joint working on the inclusion of human rights in the integration of health and social care, as well as work on health inequalities;
- work between the Scottish government and partners to put human rights at the heart of the principles which guide delivery of health and care services in Scotland, as part of the review of the National Care Standards;
- work on a HRBA to independent living, including national strategies for learning disabilities and SDS.

Implementation of SNAP is independently monitored, with regular reporting to the Scottish Parliament. The action plan ran until December 2017. At the time of writing, the SHRC is hosting a series of participatory events to bring together people and organisations from around Scotland to reflect on SNAP's successes and challenges, to guide what comes next and inform the final evaluation and report on SNAP's first four years.

A key aspect of SNAP is the promotion of a HRBA, which facilitates the integration of the norms, standards and principles of the international human rights into everyday policy and practice (SHRC, 2012). A HRBA empowers people to know and claim their rights. It increases the ability of organisations, public bodies and businesses to fulfil their human rights obligations. It also creates solid accountability, ensuring people can seek remedies when their rights are violated. HRBAs are about turning human

---

26 Available from URL: www.snaprights.info (accessed 16 February 2018).

rights from purely legal instruments into effective policies, practices and practical realities.

The PANEL principles are one way of breaking down what a HRBA means in practice. PANEL stands for:

- Participation – People should be involved in decisions that affect their rights.
- Accountability – There should be monitoring of how people's rights are being affected, as well as remedies when things go wrong.
- Non-Discrimination and Equality – All forms of discrimination must be prohibited, prevented and eliminated. People who face the biggest barriers to realising their rights should be prioritised.
- Empowerment – Everyone should understand their rights and be fully supported to take part in developing policy and practices which affect their lives.
- Legality – Approaches should be grounded in the legal rights that are set out in domestic and international laws.[27]

The SHRC has highlighted examples of good practice where organisations have applied a HRBA across health and social care. One example – C-Change Scotland – provides support to disabled people to achieve independent living. One of the people supported by the organisation stated: 'I knew I had human rights but I didn't know I had the same human rights as anybody else' (SHRC, 2016b, p. 15). The PANEL principles inform the organisation's practice in the following ways.

Participation

Individuals choose who works for them and continuously review their services to make sure they meet their needs. C-Change Scotland actively involves families, friends and communities as the foundation for support. Service users are also fundamental to continuous review of the work of the organisation as a whole.

Accountability

C-Change Scotland has a flat and accessible management structure. An Improvement Council, made up solely of service users, provides a direct link to the Board of Directors so that the organisation is accountable to those it works for.

---

27 Available from URL: http://www.scottishhumanrights.com/media/1409/shrc_hrba_ leaflet.pdf (accessed 16 February 2018).

Non-discrimination and equality

C-Change Scotland ensures that everyone is able to exercise choice in their services regardless of their level of support needs, their personal circumstances or their background. A flexible approach to support services means that those who might be marginalised by a more rigid service are able to access their rights on the same basis as others.

Empowerment

Power and control remain with, or as close to, the individual being supported, to ensure that they direct their own support. The value of their lived experience, their opinions and values are central to designing their own services and the services of the organisation.

Legality

C-Change Scotland uses the legal framework of international human rights standards to guide the services it provides and the ethos underpinning the organisation. It grounds its approach in a recognition that it exists to assist the people it works with to access their rights – to maintain family relationships, to live independently – on the same basis as others.

This organisational case study was drawn in its entirety from an SHRC report on human rights in health and social care (SHRC, 2016b, p. 16).

The PANEL principles will be used throughout this book as a reflexive tool to undertake a constructively critical analysis of legal and practice case examples.

Health and social care

Language and definitions

Social care is difficult to conceptualise as it is an umbrella term covering a very broad range of services supporting activities of everyday living. Social care services aim to help people lead as independent a life as possible. They range from supporting people to take part in social activities, help with basic personal care such as washing and dressing, through to assistance with every aspect of their daily lives. Many people access social care support, including: older people living in care homes or receiving help at home; children at risk and their families; children and adults with physical, sensory or learning disabilities; people experiencing homelessness; refugees and asylum seekers; and people with mental health problems, addictions or HIV/AIDS (Audit Scotland, 2012). Social care involves support to individuals, families and wider social networks including work with local communities. A key aspect involves supporting individuals and family members who undertake vital unpaid caring roles (Carers UK, 2015). Social care support is provided in a wide range of settings, often within an individual's home and local community, also within specialist services, and includes residential care settings. Given its disparate nature, it is unsurprising that research suggests that it is not widely understood by the public at large, many of whom are only aware of the services they have some personal experience of (The King's Fund, 2014).[28]

Social care is, however, a significant area of public expenditure. In 2014/15, councils' net expenditure on social work was £3.1 billion.[29] Net spending is total spending less income, for example from charges for services. Since 2010/11, councils' total revenue funding has reduced by 11% in real terms. Social work spending increased by 3% in real terms over the same period, and now accounts for one-third of overall council spending (Audit Scotland, 2016, p. 11). The adult social care sector in England contributes more gross value added (£20 billion) per annum to the English economy than: the production and distribution of electricity and gas (£16 billion); legal activities (£17 billion); the arts, entertainment and recreation industries (£18 billion); and the food and drink service industry (£19 billion) (Skills for Care, 2013). In Scotland, the social service workforce makes up approximately 7.7% of all Scottish employment. The three largest sub-sectors are housing support/care at home, care homes for adults and day care of children; together, these account for almost 78% of the workforce. Women make up 85% of the workforce (SSSC, 2017).

The social care sector is going through a period of significant change. The integration of health and social care and the introduction of SDS

28 The Commission on the Future of Health and Social Care England commissioned The King's Fund to write a Background Paper entitled *Attitudes to Health and Social Care. Review of Existing Research,* two of the key findings were firstly that the public has a limited understanding of the care and support system beyond their own experience (Ipsos MORI, 2009; 2011) so there is a large information gap. Secondly the general public's understanding of the distinction between health and social care is poor; there is little appreciation that social care generally is not free at the point of use like the NHS.

29 Scottish Government (February 2016) 'Scottish local government financial statistics' (online). Available from URL: www.gov.scot/Topics/Statistics/Browse/Local-Government-Finance/PubScottishLGFStats (accessed 16 February 2018).

are bringing about significant structural and procedural changes at a time of financial austerity flowing from the economic downturn in 2008. The full implications of these developments are still to be realised; there follows a brief overview to provide a context for the issues discussed in the following chapters.

Health and social care integration

Legislation to implement health and social care integration, the Public Bodies (Joint Working) (Scotland) Act, was passed by the Scottish Parliament in February 2014 and came into force on 1 April 2016.[30] This brings together NHS and local council care services under one partnership arrangement for each area. It sets out three main aims, (I) nationally agreed outcomes, which will apply across health and social care; (II) a requirement on NHS Boards and local authorities to integrate health and social care budgets; (III) a requirement on partnerships to strengthen the role of clinicians and care professionals, along with the third and independent sectors, in the planning and delivery of services.[31] The Act is designed to:

- improve the quality and consistency of services for patients, carers, service users and their families;
- provide seamless, joined-up quality health and social care services to care for people in their homes or a homely setting where it is safe to do so;
- ensure resources are used effectively and efficiently to deliver services that meet the increasing number of people with longer-term and often complex needs, many of whom are older.

In total, thirty-one local partnerships have been set up across Scotland, and they will manage almost £8 billion of health and social care resources. With such a seismic shift in the landscape of health and social care, there are significant concerns that the disruption may detract from the primary purpose of delivering high-quality health and social care. This was an issue specifically highlighted by the Audit Scotland progress report on the implementation of SDS (Audit Scotland, 2017).

---

30 Available from URL: http://www.gov.scot/Topics/Health/Policy/Adult-Health-SocialCare-Integration/About-the-Bill (accessed 16 February 2018).
31 ibid.

Self-Directed Support (SDS)

The Social Care (Self-Directed Support) (Scotland) Act 2013 came into force on 1 April 2013, heralding a significant shift in the planning, implementation and delivery of social care. The Act followed publication of the Scottish Government's ten-year national strategy for SDS in Scotland in November 2010 (Scottish Government, 2010). SDS is based on the human rights principles of fairness, respect, equality, dignity and autonomy for all.[32] It places a duty on local authority social work departments to offer people, who are eligible for social care, greater choice over how they receive their social care support.

SDS provides four options to ensure that everyone can exercise choice and control over the way they plan, organise and receive their support. The options available are:

- option 1, a direct payment (cash payment);
- option 2, funding allocated to a provider of choice (sometimes called an Individual Service Fund);
- option 3, the council will arrange the service;
- option 4, a person can choose a mix of the options available for different types of support.[33]

The implementation of SDS comes at a time when local authority budgets are under considerable strain owing to the ongoing pressures. Between 2009/10 and 2012/13, council spending on social care services decreased by 5% in real terms. At the same time, demographic changes such as an ageing population have resulted in increased demand for social services.[34] The economic climate provides a challenging context for the realisation of the human rights aspirations inherent within the Social Care (Self-Directed Support) (Scotland) Act.

A UN Convention on the Rights of Persons with Disabilities Committee report in 2016 made critical reference to the implementation of personalised budgets for social care in the UK.[35] It noted that:

32 The Human Rights Act 1998.
33 Available from URL: http://selfdirectedsupportscotland.org.uk (accessed 16 February 2018).
34 Scottish Local Government Financial Statistics 2012–13, Scottish Government, 2014, in Audit Scotland: Self Directed Support, June 2014.
35 Committee on the Rights of Persons with Disabilities, Inquiry concerning the United Kingdom of Great Britain and Northern Ireland carried out by the Committee under Article 6 of the Optional Protocol to the Convention, Report of the Committee, CRPD/C/15/R.2/Rev.1., 2016.

it had received evidence that personal care packages have been reduced and that the availability of support is established on the basis of what is considered to be an affordable service in the market, rather than the specific needs of the person concerned.[36]

An unintended consequence of SDS implementation has been a rise in applications for welfare guardianship orders (substitute decision-making), particularly in relation to young people with a learning disability (MWC, 2016b). It has also been argued that the implementation of personalisation through the introduction of SDS has placed little emphasis on human rights. In the absence of a robust human rights framework, SDS has failed to address the systemic power imbalance and has continued to deliver not necessarily what people need but what the system can deliver (Chetty *et al.*, 2012). Adoption of an HRBA has the potential to override the economic rationalist agendas common in much social care today (Skegg, 2005).

Putting rights into practice

In this challenging context, a HRBA can offer a bulwark against the worst excesses of austerity. It provides those who use services and professionals who work in the field with a simple guide to navigate the difficult terrain of competing demand and priorities. Indeed, the International Federation of Social Work was unequivocal in stating that the principle of human rights is by its very definition intrinsic to social work (Hare, 2004). The main aim of social care is to assist people who require support to live their idea of a good life. 'A good life' is a life lived in accordance with an individual's fundamental beliefs about what is important and valuable, in which they can formulate plans and realise them. Living a good life gives individuals a sense of identity and purpose (Connolly, 2008). Adopting a HRBA can help ensure that the focus person remains at the centre of any planned support.

Some commentators have noted an increasing fragmentation of human rights along group lines, children, women, persons with disabilities, indigenous peoples, migrants and asylum seekers (Mégret, 2008, p. 494). The format of this book reflects this fragmentation but

---

36 ibid.

only as a narrative device which enables detailed analysis of the issues experienced by, in turn, children, women, disabled people and older persons. It is important to recognise the concept of intersectionality, that individuals experience overlapping layers of disadvantage and discrimination that cannot be simplified into a preconceived hierarchy of disadvantage. The chapter structure is not intended to support singular descriptions of identity.

Chapter 2, The Rights of the Child, explores the international development of the human rights of the child, specifically the UN Convention on the Rights of the Child (UNCRC). Consideration is given to the influence of international developments on UK domestic legislation, policy and practice and the consequent implications for social care. Attention is paid to some unique aspects of law, policy and practice in Scotland. This chapter explores the contentious issue of competing rights and provides legal and case examples to illustrate the benefit of adopting an HRBA.

Chapter 3, The Rights of Women, explores the development of human rights as it relates to women. It charts the evolution from the early gender-neutral conception of human rights through to the development of the Convention on the Elimination of All Forms of Discrimination Against Women (CEDAW). The issue of domestic violence is used as a thematic example to illustrate the evolving jurisprudence of the ECHR. Legal and practice case studies are used to illustrate the benefits of adopting a HRBA.

Chapter 4, The Rights of Disabled People, explores the development of human rights protections for disabled people internationally and nationally. The UN Convention on the Rights of Persons with Disabilities (CRPD) has outlined a clear direction for the enhancement of the lives of disabled persons. The Convention offers a challenge to domestic legislation, policy and practice, particularly in respect of the issue of legal and mental capacity. Legal and practice case studies are used to illustrate the potential in adopting an HRBA based upon the PANEL principles.

Chapter 55, The Rights of Older Persons, explores the benefits of adopting an HRBA in social care for older citizens. Unlike the social groups discussed in Chapters 2, 3 and 4, there is no UN Convention on the rights of older persons, although there is a concerted campaign to establish such an international human rights instrument. In the absence of a Convention, the discussion focuses on the specific human rights violations experienced by older persons and offers examples of legal and practice case studies, working within the current legislative framework, that illustrate the benefits of adopting an HRBA.

The book's conclusion pulls together the main themes emerging from the preceding chapters and offers a potential way forward.

Conclusion

Human rights crises initially emerge at the local level. It is at the local level that abuses occur, and where a first line of defence needs to be developed, first and foremost by those who are under threat (de Feyter and Parmentier, 2011). It is at the local level that human rights are either real or illusory. People who use social care and their families and those who work in social care, both at an individual and an organisational level, can be daunted by the legalistic and often adversarial interpretation of human rights and what people need to do to claim them. An HRBA, using the PANEL principles, can help navigate and negotiate the complexity of competing interests and claims. The credibility and effectiveness of global human rights rest with their local relevance and the appropriation of international norms and mechanisms by those whose rights are continually violated at a local level. This implies that local people and communities should be able to participate in the human rights struggle at all levels and to see the impact of human rights in practice (de Feyter and Parmentier, 2011, p. 4). One of the aims of this book is to illustrate the potential of the HRBA as a practical tool that can be used when making difficult decisions in a time of 'austerity'. Human rights provide an effective framework, grounded in law, that can ensure the advancement of human dignity is at the heart of social care policy and practice decisions:

> Human dignity follows from listening closely to what it is that people truly value and allowing them the opportunity to translate their vision of what constitutes a good life into a reality (Connolly, 2008, p. 12).

Eleanor Roosevelt, the Chair of the inaugural United Nations Commission on Human Rights, expressed a desire that a 'curious grapevine' would carry the idea of human rights into every corner of the world, offering the normative framework of the UDHR as an alternative to the existing innumerable diversity of rule systems. This book aims to add one small branch to that ever expanding 'curious grapevine'.

CHAPTER 2

The Rights of the Child

*with Juliet Harris**

*Juliet Harris, Director of Together (Scottish Alliance for Children's Rights), leads the organisation in promoting and monitoring the implementation of the UN Convention on the Rights of the Child (UNCRC) across Scotland.

> … I am convinced that the great mass of our people go through life without even a glimmer of what they could have contributed to their fellow human beings. This is a personal tragedy. It is a social crime. The flowering of each individual's personality and talents is the pre-condition for everyone's development (Reid, 1972, p. 11).

Introduction

As we have already established in Chapter 1, human rights are universal, they apply to people of all ages; children have the same basic rights as adults. Children require additional levels of care and protection and for specific rights to be realised for them to develop their full potential. These rights are enshrined in international law in the UN Convention on the Rights of the Child (UNCRC). As previously outlined, the Scottish Parliament was created by the Scotland Act 1998.[1] Its powers were extended by the Scotland Act 2012[2] and further amended by the Scotland Act 2016.[3] Certain matters relating to children's rights were devolved to the Scottish Parliament and government, and these include education and training, health and social services, housing and local government. The

---

1 Scotland Act 1998. Available from URL: http://www.legislation.gov.uk/ukpga/1998/46/contents (accessed 16 February 2018).
2 Scotland Act 2012. Available from URL: http://www.legislation.gov.uk/ukpga/2012/11/contents/enacted (accessed 16 February 2018).
3 Available from URL: http://www.legislation.gov.uk/ukpga/2016/11/contents/enacted (accessed 16 February 2018).

Scottish Parliament established Scotland's Commissioner for Children and Young People in 2003,[4] with a function to 'promote and safeguard the rights of children and young people' with reference to the UNCRC[5] (SHRC, 2013, p. 17).

There is no singular experience of childhood or being a child. All children, including gypsy/traveller children, disabled children, children from minority ethnic backgrounds, child carers, looked-after and care-experienced children, migrant, asylum-seeking and refugee children, lesbian, gay, transgender and intersex children, young women and girls, have multiple facets that make them who they are. Recognising intersectionality[6] and the importance of the different dimensions of each child's unique experience is fundamental to respecting, promoting and protecting the rights of all children in Scotland.

Discussions around the human rights of children are often framed in terms of striking a balance between the rights of the child, the rights of parents and the needs of the wider community. The UNCRC includes the rights of parents as well as the rights of children. It outlines the role of parents in guaranteeing and promoting the rights of the child and is clear that the State should provide parents with the necessary level of support they need to fulfil their role.[7] Through this interpretation, the UNCRC intends to resolve any perceived tensions between the rights of children and the rights of their parents. The role of parents in guaranteeing the rights of the child needs to be seen in the context of encouraging respect for children's evolving capacity to exercise their rights as they acquire competence to do so.[8] In practice, this means ensuring the fullest possible protection to all children from harm while encouraging and nurturing their right to be involved in decisions that affect their lives. This balancing act has provoked controversy in many

---

4 Commissioner for Children and Young People (Scotland) Act 2003. Available from URL: http://www.legislation.gov.uk/asp/2003/17 (accessed 16 February 2018)

5 2003 Act, s.4 and s.5.

6 Defined by the *Oxford English Dictionary* as: 'The interconnected nature of social categorizations such as race, class, and gender as they apply to a given individual or group, regarded as creating overlapping and interdependent systems of discrimination or disadvantage'. Available from URL: https://en.oxforddictionaries.com/definition/intersectionality (accessed 16 February 2018).

7 UNCRC Article 18.

8 UNCRC Article 5.

areas of children's rights, such as healthcare[9] and justice[10], as well as pervaded family law and almost all services associated with children including education and social care.

Space does not allow for a full exposition of the diversity of children's experiences and the associated human rights challenges of growing up in Scotland. The focus of this chapter is the issue of children's human rights in the field of social care and how these rights can be incorporated into practice. There is a notable lack of clearly identifiable jurisprudence in relation to human rights, social care and children in Scotland. Legal cases and practice examples in this area are frequently framed within a health or education paradigm; consequently, examples in this chapter have been drawn from this wider ambit, with consideration for their relevance to the field of social care. The PANEL principles of participation, accountability, non-discrimination, empowerment and legality will be used as a reflexive tool to analyse legal and practice examples to illustrate the applicability of an HRBA in practice. Before examining the historical development of the human rights of children, it is first necessary to consider the issues of definition and demography.

Language, definition and demographics

The age range that constitutes being a child can appear confusing, with different age restrictions applied to certain activities such as voting, marrying and joining the armed forces. The UNCRC states:

> For the purposes of the present Convention, a child means every human being below the age of eighteen years unless under the law applicable to the child, majority is attained earlier.[11]

In Scotland, the Children's Commissioner is responsible for protecting the rights of young people up to the age of twenty-one if they have been looked after or in care. A child or young person does not need to be a Scottish citizen to fall under the Commissioner's protection; they must just live in Scotland.[12]

---

9 SL (Permission to Vaccinate), Re 2017 EWHC (Fam) EWHC (30 January 2017) [2017] EWHC 125 (Fam); C v. A (A Minor) [2011] EWHC 4033 (Fam).

10 For example, the debate around increasing the age of criminal responsibility. Available from URL: https://consult.gov.scot/youth-justice/minimum-age-of-criminal-responsibility (accessed 16 February 2018).

11 UNCRC Article 1.

12 Available from URL: www.cypcs.org.uk/rights/uncrcarticles/article-1 (accessed 16 February 2018).

In June 2014, there were 1,031,761 children (under eighteen years old) in Scotland. Of these, 227,497 children were aged 0–3 years and 528,254 children were aged 0–8.[13] Across Scotland, 17.5 per 1,000 under eighteens are looked after or on the child protection register (Scottish Government, 2014b). The decision to place a child's name on the register takes place following a Child Protection Case Conference where there are reasonable grounds to believe or suspect that a child has suffered or will suffer significant harm from abuse or neglect, and that a Child Protection Plan is needed to protect and support the child (Scottish Government, 2014c).

Considerable variation in numbers exists across local authorities; in general, rates are higher in the west of Scotland and urban areas (Scottish Government, 2017b). [14] Over the last ten years, children have started to be looked after at a younger age. In 2005, 29% of children starting to be looked after were aged under five. By 2016, this had risen to 38%. A large proportion of this group are the under one year olds, and the numbers in this youngest group have almost doubled since 2005. There was a corresponding decrease in the proportion of children aged twelve plus being looked after, while those in the 5–11 age group remained stable.[15] According to the 2011 census, boys make up 51% of the population under eighteen. Of those children starting to be looked after, 54% were boys (Scottish Government, 2017b). The number of young people in secure care accommodation on 31 July 2015 was eighty-eight, just under 40% of whom were aged sixteen years and over. Those leaving care are more likely to have poor educational outcomes and low levels of access to further education and to experience low employment or unemployment (Reed in Partnership, 2011). This includes higher levels of offending, with one-third of young offenders identified as having been in care and nearly one-third of adult

---

13 National Records of Scotland. Available from URL: www.nrscotland.gov.uk/statistics-and-data/statistics/statistics-by-theme/population/population-estimates (accessed 16 February 2018).

14 In 2014 in the adult population the largest ethnic group was 'white: Scottish' at 77.9%, adults from minority ethnic groups represented 3.4% of the population. At 31 July 2016, 88% of all children looked after were reported as being from a 'White' ethnic group, with a further 4% being from 'Mixed Ethnicity', 'Asian, Asian Scottish or Asian British', 'Black, Black Scottish or Black British' or 'Other' ethnic groups. Note that 8% were reported as having a 'Not Disclosed/Not Known' ethnic group. Available from URL: http://www.gov.scot/Topics/People/Equality/Equalities/DataGrid/Ethnicity (accessed 16 February 2018).

15 *supra* n. 13.

prisoners, 31%, also self-reported being in care as a child (SPS, 2016). Research indicates higher levels of mental ill health, with 45% of children and young people (aged 5–17) looked-after by a local authority having a diagnosable mental disorder (Meltzer *et al.*, 2004). Lower levels of educational attainment have also been highlighted, with 73% of looked after young people leaving school before the age of sixteen compared with 27% of all school leavers. Only 35% of care-experienced young people leave with one or more qualifications at Scottish Credit and Qualifications Framework (SCQF) level 5, whereas 85% of all school leavers achieve this level, and only 4% of looked-after young people were recorded as going straight on to higher education, compared to 39% of their non-looked-after peers (Scottish Government, 2015). Care leavers are also more likely to experience poorer life outcomes (Elsley *et al.*, 2007).

The Scottish government does not currently have information on levels of disability in relation to children and families. Information that was previously labelled as 'disability' does not meet the definition of disability outlined in the Equality Act 2010 and is more accurately described as additional support needs.[16] In 2015/16, after housing costs were taken account, 260,000 or 26% of children in Scotland were living in relative poverty. This compares to 22% in 2014/15 (Scottish Government, 2016a, p. 13). This level of child poverty is significantly higher than in many other European countries.[17] While childhood poverty shares causes and manifestations with poverty experienced by adults, there are some important differences in effects. Crucially, childhood poverty may have lifelong consequences (Marshall, 2003).

Historical development of the rights of the child

In 1924, the League of Nations adopted a Declaration on the Rights of the Child (Declaration of Geneva) containing five basic principles reflecting the clear consensus that children were in need of special protection.[18] In 1959, the UN General Assembly unanimously adopted another more

---

16 Available from URL: http://www.gov.scot/Topics/People/Equality/Equalities/ DataGrid/disability/disabChYP (accessed 16 February 2018).

17 International comparisons are for 2011 on a before housing-costs basis, under which 15% of Scotland's children live in poverty, taken from Child Poverty Action Group in Scotland. Available from URL: http://www.cpag.org.uk/scotland/child-poverty-facts-and-figures (accessed 16 February 2017).

18 Available from URL: http://www.un-documents.net/gdrc1924.htm (accessed 16 February 2018).

elaborate Declaration on the Rights of the Child, stating in the preamble that 'the child, by reason of his physical and mental immaturity, needs special safeguards and care, including appropriate legal protection, before as well as after birth'.[19]

Serious work on drafting a Convention on the rights of the child began in the final years of the 1970s, resulting in the UN General Aassembly adoption of the Convention on the Rights of the Child (UNCRC) on 20 November 1989.[20] The Convention came into force on 2 September 1990 and, at October 2017, 196 states had ratified it, making the UNCRC the most universally accepted human rights treaty ever drafted. The United States is the only UN member which is not party to the Convention.

UN Convention on the Rights of the Child (UNCRC)

The UNCRC is sometimes referred to as the most complete of the international human rights instruments, including as it does civil, political, economic, social and cultural rights. It shies away from distinguishing between these rights, instead underlining their universality, indivisibility and interdependence. The UNCRC drafting process involved more than fifty State parties and took eleven years (Cantwell, 1992) and, as a result, it includes several compromises. For example, it sets no minimum age of criminal responsibility nor minimum age of marriage, although these issues, among others, have been addressed through General Comments and Concluding Observations from the UN Committee on the Rights of the Child (Johnson, 1992). Furthermore, elements of the Convention itself reflect what could be considered as outdated approaches to human rights. UNCRC Article 23 has been criticised for presenting an outdated medical model of disability rather than the social model included in the more recent UN Convention on the Rights of Persons with Disabilities (CRPD). The model of non-discrimination enshrined in Article 2 could be more meaningfully portrayed through the lens of equality (Freeman, 2000).

The Convention has fifty-four Articles and is meant to be all-encompassing. It sets out civil, political, social, economic and cultural rights for

19 Declaration of the Rights of the Child (1959), G.A. res. 1386 (XIV), 14 UN GAOR Supp. (No. 16) at 19, UN Doc. A/4354.
20 Adopted and opened for signature, ratification and accession by General Assembly resolution 44/25 of 20 November 1989.

'every human being below the age of eighteen years, unless under the law applicable to the child, majority is attained earlier' (Article 1). The Convention must be seen as a whole with all rights linked and no right more important that another. Four general principles guided the authors of the Convention:

- the principle of non-discrimination (Article 2);
- the best interests of the child (Article 3);
- the right to life, survival and development (Article 6);
- respect for the views of the child (Article 12).

Underpinning the UNCRC are three core concepts – protection, provision and participation: (1) protection against, e.g., violence, abuse, neglect, maltreatment or exploitation (Article 19); (2) provision of, e.g., name and nationality (Article 7), social security, adequate standard of living and education (Articles 26 to 28); and (3) participation through the right of a child to express its views, to freedom of thought and to freedom of association (Articles 12 to 15).

The UNCRC contains several rights which are also included in other international instruments, but Article 41 provides an explicit 'most favourable conditions clause', stating that nothing in the UNCRC shall affect any provisions which are more conducive to the realisation of the rights of the child and which may be contained in the law of a State party or international law in force in that State (Article 41). While the Convention sets out many rights already proclaimed in other instruments, such as the ICCPR (Articles 23(4) and 24) and the ICESCR (Article 10(3)), it is the first instrument to specifically grant children rights and protection as autonomous human beings. The value added by the UNCRC lies mainly in the following:

- The general rights formulated in earlier Conventions and the UDHR have been reformulated with a special focus on the rights and needs of the child. Other rights only applicable to children are elaborated, such as the right to adoption, education and contact with parents.
- New elements have been included, such as the provisions regarding parental guidance and international cooperation in relation to disabled children.
- The UNCRC covers children in difficult circumstances, such as the separation from parents; abuse and neglect; disabled and refugee children; indigenous children and children belonging to minorities;

sale, trafficking and abduction of children; deprivation of liberty; and children in armed conflict.

Some international instruments contain more protective clauses than the UNCRC. For example, Article 32 UNCRC regarding child labour does not explicitly define a minimum age for admission to employment. The International Labour Organisation (ILO) Convention 138 stipulates that the minimum age for admission to employment or work shall not be less than fifteen years although developing countries may initially specify a minimum age of fourteen years.[21] Similarly, while the UNCRC forbids recruitment of children below fifteen years for the armed forces, Article 77 of Protocol I to the Geneva Conventions of 1949[22] affords superior protection as regards recruitment of children between fifteen and seventeen years of age. Furthermore, the Optional Protocol to the UNCRC on the involvement of children in armed conflict (2002) built on the original provisions of the UNCRC to provide that no one under the age of eighteen takes a direct part in hostilities or is compulsorily recruited into the armed forces.[23] Here, Article 41 ('most favourable treatment') applies for those States which are parties to more favourable international instruments.

UNCRC monitoring and oversight

The UNCRC establishes the Committee on the Rights of the Child (CRC) to supervise the progress made by the States parties in achieving the realisation of their obligations under the Convention. The Committee is composed of eighteen experts from fields such as international law, medicine, education and sociology, whose main task is to review reports submitted by States on actions they have taken to implement the Convention, as it has no competence to receive individual complaints. The Committee may convene informal regional meetings with the collaboration of Unicef, to familiarise itself with the specific issues facing children in different regions, as well as establishing dialogues with non-governmental organisations (NGOs) and governments.

---

21 Convention concerning Minimum Age for Admission to Employment, C138 – Minimum Age Convention, 1973 (No. 138) (Entry into force: 19 June 1976).

22 Available from URL: www.icrc.org/eng/assets/files/other/icrc_002_0321.pdf (accessed 16 February 2018).

23 Optional Protocol to the Convention on the Rights of the Child on the involvement of children in armed conflict (Entry into force: 12 February 2002) (Articles 1 and 2). Available from URL: www.ohchr.org/EN/ProfessionalInterest/Pages/OPACCRC.aspx (accessed 16 February 2018).

As with other supervisory mechanisms, the Committee adopts General Comments for the interpretation of the rights contained in the UNCRC. To date, the Committee has adopted twenty-one General Comments. For example, General Comment 5 on general measures of implementation of the UNCRC; General Comment 6 on the treatment of unaccompanied and separated children from their country of origin; General Comment 8 on corporal, and other cruel or degrading forms of punishment; General Comment 9 on the rights of children with disabilities;[24] and General Comment 10 on juvenile justice.

International Covenant on Civil and Political Rights (ICCPR) – Human Rights Committee (HRC)

The HRC is the body of independent experts that monitors implementation of the ICCPR by its State parties. The HRC has also been active in the protection of children. The following cases have potential implications in the field of social care and illustrate the Committee's approach.

The Committee has, for example, set out that the exceptional circumstances that limit the right to regular contact between children and both of their parents upon dissolution of a marriage generally does not include unilateral opposition of one parent, *Hendriks v. The Netherlands*.[25] The failure of the State to ensure the right to permanent contact between a divorced parent and her children entailed an interference with the right to privacy, *Fei v. Colombia*.[26] The deportation of parents from a country where a child has nationality and has grown up constitutes an arbitrary interference with the right to family, as well as a violation of the child's right to special protection as a minor, *Hendrick Winata and Li v. Australia*.[27] A violation arose because of unreasonably long child custody proceedings between a parent and a State authority (attempting to place a child into foster care). To determine whether a delay is reasonable or unreasonable, domestic courts must weigh the

---

24 General Comment No. 9 (2006) on the rights of children with disabilities defines disability using the social model included in the CRPD and 'emphasizes that the barrier is not the disability itself but rather a combination of social, cultural, attitudinal and physical obstacles which children with disabilities encounter in their daily lives' (para 5). Available from URL: http://tbinternet.ohchr.org/_layouts/treatybodyexternal/Download.aspx?symbolno=CRC%2fC%2fGC%2f9&Lang=en (accessed 16 February 2018)..

25 *Hendriks v. Netherlands* (1982) 5 EHRR 223

26 *Fei v. Colombia* (1995) Merits, IHRL 2243, UNHRC.

27 *Hendrick Winata and So Lan Li v. Australia* (2001) UNHRC.

age of the child at the centre of proceedings, the possible impact on the well-being of the child, and the overall outcome of the case, *Ms Natalya Tcholatch v. Canada*.[28]

European Convention on Human Rights (ECHR)

As outlined in Chapter 1, the ECHR guarantees civil and political rights and is applicable to adults and children.[29] It makes very little mention of children within its provisions (Grant and Sutherland, 2009), which is largely a reflection of the norms of its 1950s' origins, and omits the social, economic and cultural rights that are such an intrinsic part of the UNCRC. This has led to debate as to whether it risks failing to take account of children's dependent and vulnerable status (Marshall, 2009). Despite such concerns, the ECHR has made a substantial contribution to the advancement of children's rights.[30] The UNCRC has been ratified by all member states of the Council of Europe and therefore binds all States party to the ECHR. As a result, the UNCRC has usefully informed case law, with the ECtHR describing the UNCRC as setting out 'the human rights of children and the standards to which all governments must aspire in realising these rights for all children'.[31] Article 8(1) provides that 'everyone has the right to respect for his private and family life, his home and his correspondence'. Article 8(2) then prohibits the State from interfering with this right unless such interference is justified on one of the grounds set out in Article 8(2). The right to respect for family life is, therefore, a qualified and not an absolute right; interferences by the State must be in accordance with the law, be necessary in a democratic society and proportionate to certain legitimate aims. These include: the interests of national security, public safety or the economic well-being of the country; the prevention of disorder or crime; the protection of health or morals; or the protection of the rights and freedoms of others. Compliance with

---

28 *Ms Natalya Tcholatch v. Canada* (2007) UNHRC.

29 ECHR Article 1 requires State Parties to 'secure to everyone within their jurisdiction the rights and freedoms defined in Section I'.

30 For an in-depth study see: Kilkelly, U. (1999) *The Child and the ECHR*, Aldershot: Ashgate; Kilkelly, U. (2001) 'The best of both worlds for children's rights: Interpreting the European CRC on Human Rights in the light of the UN Convention on the Rights of the Child', *Human Rights Quarterly*, Vol. 23, No. 2, pp. 308–26. For a more current study see: Kilkelly, U. (2015) 'The CRC in litigation under the ECHR', in Liefaard, T. and Doek, J. (2015) *Litigating the Rights of the Child*, Dordrecht: Springer, pp. 193—210.

31 *Sommerfeld v. Germany* (2004) 38 EHRR 35, at 37.

ECHR Article 8 requires a fair balance to be achieved between the competing rights and interests of parents, children and wider society.[32] In striking such a balance, particular importance must be attached to the welfare of the child which, depending on their nature and seriousness, may override the rights of the parent.[33]

European Court of Human Rights (ECtHR)

The jurisprudence of the ECtHR is clear that State parties must take positive action to secure the rights of its citizens[34] as well as abstaining from certain actions.[35] The ECtHR uses the UNCRC as an aid to interpret the ECHR.[36] ECHR Articles 3 and 8 are the source of the majority of ECtHR jurisprudence relating to children. ECHR Article 14, the non-discrimination principle, can be invoked only in relation to an additional ECHR right. It has, nevertheless, proved to be important: age is a ground on which discrimination is prohibited, and Article 14 has been found to place a positive obligation to secure ECHR rights without discrimination.[37]

The establishment of positive obligations under the ECHR has played an instrumental role in cases relating to contact, custody and access (in relation to ECHR Article 8) and has been important in cases relating to child protection and abuse, in relation to ECHR Article 3 (Kilkelly, 2015). In Scotland, *Z and others v. UK* established that there is a positive obligation to protect children from ill-treatment about which it had, or ought to have, knowledge in line with UNCRC Article 19.[38] It

---

32 Article 8(1), see: *Hokkanen v. Finland* (1994) 19 EHRR 139 Article 8(2), see: *Maumousseau and Washington v. France* [2007] ECHR 1204, (2010) 51 EHRR 35. In a controversial case, the ECtHR set out that the best interests of the child should be the paramount consideration, going further than UNCRC Article 3, see: *Neulinger and Shuruk v. Switzerland* [2010] ECHR 1053.

33 *Johansen v. Norway* (1996) 23 EHRR 33 para 78.

34 *Marckx v. Belgium* (1979) 14 EHRR 330 was a landmark case in this matter in which the ECtHR ruled that all legal impediments to an illegitimate child being a member of the mother's family must be removed to secure the applicant's ECHR Article 8 right to family life.

35 For example, abstaining from torture (ECHR Article 3).

36 This was reinforced in *Sahin v. Germany* (2003) 36 EHRR 43, para 39: 'The human rights of children and the standards to which all governments must aspire in realising these rights for all children are set out in the Convention on the Rights of the Child'.

37 See Belgian Linguistic case (No. 2) (1968) 1 EHRR 252 in which it was found that there was no obligation to provide a particular education system, but, when it was chosen to do so, access could not be restricted in a discriminatory manner.

38 *Z and others v. UK* (2001) 34 EHRR 31.

is worth noting that, if the Article 3 threshold for degrading treatment is not reached, a victim may still have a right to a remedy under Article 8, which also covers the integrity of the person (Finch and McGroarty, 2014). *E and others v. UK* found a violation of ECHR Articles 3 and 13 in relation to the failure of a local authority to protect children from serious abuse by their stepfather and found the remedies for historic child abuse to be inadequate.[39] While children's rights have been progressed through the establishment of such positive obligations, much has relied on the interpretive powers of the ECtHR, which can make outcomes 'difficult to predict' (Kilkelly, 2015, p. 196).

The ECtHR can be used to challenge legislation that is seen to be in direct contravention of children's rights, where they relate to the ECHR. The ECtHR's recognition of the 'living instrument' doctrine has supported the development of case law to reflect 'current legal and social conditions'.[40] Beginning in 1978 with *Tyrer v. UK*, the ECtHR ruled that the birching of a child was a degrading punishment and in violation of ECHR Article 3.[41] Soon after, *Campbell and Cosans v. UK* resulted in corporal punishment being banned from local authority schools.[42] *Costello-Roberts v. UK* established that, in order for a punishment to be in breach of ECHR Article 3, it had to attain a particular level of severity, the assessment of which depended on the circumstances of the case.[43] *A v. UK* found the defence of 'reasonable chastisement' permitted in law a violation of ECHR Article 3.[44] In making this judgement, the Commission had particular regard to UNCRC Articles 19 and 37. As a result, the UK and Scottish governments were required to amend domestic law accordingly, in order to remain compliant with their ECHR obligations.

Despite the influence of ECtHR judgements, legislation in Scotland provides that parents who assault their child can still advance a defence of 'justifiable assault' if they claim the action was 'physical punishment

---

39 *E and others v. UK* (2003) 36 EHRR 31.

40 Established in *Tyrer v. UK*, App. No. 5856/72 (1978) 2 EHRR 1, [1978] ECHR 2.

41 ibid., para 31.

42 Whilst this case was brought to the Court in relation to Article 3, the Court did not find a breach as the child had not received corporal punishment. However, it found the UK in breach of the ECHR Article 2 Protocol 1 by not respecting parents' objections to school corporal punishment. *Campbell and Cosans v. UK* (1982) 4 EHRR 293.

43 *Costello-Roberts v. UK* (1995) 19 EHRR 112.

44 *A v. UK* (1999) 27 EHRR 611.

carried out in the exercise of a parental right' and was justifiable.[45] The Committee has published a General Comment on the issue[46] and, along with the Human Rights Council,[47] has made numerous observations that this is a violation of UNCRC Article 19. It is argued that, if a case were to be presented today, the ECtHR may rule the defence for corporal punishment as being contrary to ECHR Article 3.[48] This highlights the limitations of using the ECtHR to tackle the gaps in protection of UNCRC rights: the ECtHR can only use the UNCRC to interpret rather than enforce ECHR rights, and cases rely on a child's rights being violated before they can be brought to the ECtHR.

Lastly, two 2008 cases from Finland demonstrate the vigilance of the court when it comes to the concept of 'child protection'. The applicant in *Juppala v. Finland*[49] was a grandparent who raised a fear of child abuse with a doctor while her grandchild was having a bruise examined. The doctor referred the matter to child welfare. The child's father was cleared of any wrongdoing and brought and succeeded in an action for defamation against the applicant. The court was troubled by the use of defamation in this way. The court was especially worried by the 'chilling effect' the decision could have on the reporting of child abuse. In *K.U. v. Finland*,[50] the court dealt with the lack of criminal investigation into a breach of a twelve year old's Internet privacy rights. An anonymous person had posted a fake advertisement with the applicant's name, age, photo and telephone number (save for one incorrect digit) asking for an intimate relationship 'to show him the way'. The police could not compel the service provider to reveal the identity of the advertisement's

---

45 Criminal Justice (Scotland) Act 2003, s.51(1). The defence can also be used by those who claim the action was in exercise of a 'right derived from having charge or care of a child'.

46 Committee on the Rights of the Child, 2006. General Comment No. 8: The Right of the Child to Protection from Corporal Punishment and Other Cruel and Degrading Forms of Punishment.

47 Committee on the Rights of the Child (1995) para 16; *supra* 12 (2002), para 38; (2008) paras 40–4; and Human Rights Council (2012) recs 110.78, 110.79, 110.80.

48 Bruce Adamson blog (2014) 'The need for equal protection from violence for children in Scottish criminal law', British Association for Child and Adolescent Public Health. Available from URL: www.bacaph.org.uk/blog/52-blog-item1-12 (accessed 12 March 2018. *Opinion of Senior Counsel re the Legality of Scots Law on the Physical Punishment of Children* was commissioned by the Children's Rights Strategic Litigation Working Group on Equal Protection. Available from URL: www.togetherscotland.org.uk/pdfs/Legal_Opinion_Janys_Scott_QC.pdf (accessed 16 February 2018).

49 *Juppala v. Finland* (2008) ECtHR.

50 *K.U. v. Finland* (2008) ECtHR.

creator. The Finnish legislature was deemed to be in breach of Article 8 for failing to put in place a legal framework capable of adequately balancing general privacy rights with the privacy rights of children.

The rights of the child in the UK

It is the UK, rather than Scotland, that is State party to any international treaty and the power to ratify, withdraw or amend international treaties lies at a UK level.[51] The UK ratified the UNCRC in 1991. According to the rules of international law, the UNCRC is legally binding on every State that is party to it.[52] As previously detailed in Chapter 1, the UK constitution is based upon a 'dualist approach' whereby international agreements are not incorporated into domestic law until legislation is passed which explicitly incorporates, such as the Human Rights Act 1998. Children and young people, therefore, are unable at present to directly protect their UNCRC rights through the domestic courts as it has not been incorporated into domestic UK or Scots law. It is presumed that Parliament does not intend to legislate in a manner that is incompatible with international treaties to which the UK is a party, and these treaties can still be used as an aid to the construction of domestic law.[53]

Human Rights Act 1998 (HRA)

As previously detailed in Chapter 1, the HRA incorporates much of the ECHR into UK law.[54] It gives adults and children the ability to protect

---

51 The Constitutional Reform and Governance Act 2010 provides that treaties cannot be ratified unless they have been laid before the UK Parliament for twenty-one days without either House having resolved that it should not be ratified. The UK and devolved governments administrations have agreed concordats which include the formulation of UK policy and implementation of international obligations. See Foreign and Commonwealth Office (2014) *Treaties and Memoranda of Understanding: Guidance on Practice and Procedures*, London: Foreign and Commonwealth Office. Available from URL: www.gov.uk/government/uploads/system/uploads/attachment_data/file/293976/ Treaties_and_MoU_Guidance.pdf (accessed 12 March 2018)

52 Vienna Convention on the Law of Treaties (1969), Article 26: 'Every treaty in force is binding upon the parties to it and must be performed by them in good faith'. Article 31(1): a treaty 'shall be interpreted in good faith in accordance with the ordinary meaning to be given to the terms of the treaty in their context and in the light of its object and purpose'.

53 *Shields v. Shields* 2002 SC 246 (p. 248): 'The United Kingdom became a signatory to the United Nations Convention [on the Rights of the Child] on 16 December 1991 and it was not in dispute that the Convention could be used as an aid to construction of the domestic legislation which later sought to implement it and which, for present purposes, is to be found in sec 11(7)(b) of the Children (Scotland) Act 1995'.

54 The HRA 1998 does not incorporate every ECHR Article: s.1 defines the ECHR rights to

their ECHR rights through the domestic courts and includes a range of provisions to ensure the realisation of ECHR rights. Domestic courts are required to take account of the case law of the ECtHR.[55] All laws must be understood as far as possible in a manner compatible with the rights contained in the HRA.[56] Public authorities must refrain from acting incompatibly with the rights in the HRA.[57] The HRA applies to all public bodies, including the UK and Scottish governments and the courts. It has been applied in a series of legal cases affecting children and young people: for example, in *R (W) v. Commissioner of Police*[58] the human rights organisation Liberty brought a case on behalf of a four-teen-year-old W, challenging the police's power to take young people under the age of sixteen home from designated areas if they were out after 9pm, under the Anti-Social Behaviour Act 2003. Liberty relied on W's rights under Articles 5, 8 and 14 (rights to liberty, private life and right not to be discriminated against). The court ruled that the power in the Anti-Social Behaviour Act 2003 to use force to 'remove' a person under sixteen could only be used to remove children who are involved in, or at risk from, actual or imminently anticipated anti-social behaviour. It did not confer a power to remove law-abiding children simply because they were in a designated area at night (Human Rights Futures Project, 2011, p. 2).

In another example, *R (Williamson) v. Secretary of State for Education,*[59] the court found that the right to religion did not allow corporal punishment in private schools. Recognising that the ban on corporal punishment in schools interfered with parents' and teachers' right to manifest their religion (under Article 9), the court found that this interference was necessary in a democratic society for the protection of the rights of children (Human Rights Futures Project, 2011, p. 3). A growing number of cases place considerable emphasis on Articles in the UNCRC.[60] As such, the

which effect is given as ECHR Articles 2–12 and 14; Articles 1 and 3 Protocol 1, Articles 1 and 3 Protocol 6, and Article 1 Protocol 13, as read with ECHR Articles 16–18.

55 HRA 1998, s.2. A duty to take account is not the same as a duty to follow. See, for example, *R v. Horncastle* [2009] UKSC 14.

56 HRA 1998, s.3. Lord Hope stated in *DS v. HM Advocate* 2008 SCCR 929 para 24: 'the obligation to construe a provision in an act of the Scottish Parliament so far as it is possible to do so in a way that is compatible with the Convention rights is a strong one'.

57 HRA 1998, s.6.

58 *R (W) v. Commissioner of Police for the Metropolis and others* [2006] EWCA Civ 458.

59 *R (Williamson) v. Secretary of State for Education and Employment* [2005] UKHL 15.

60 See *ZH (Tanzania) v. Secretary of State for the Home Department* [2011] UKSC4

Convention has had a significant impact on Scottish child law (Sutherland and Cleland, 2009).

Application of the human rights agenda is not consistent. Although the ECHR has been integrated into domestic law through the HRA, its entitlements are not consistently promoted in social policy.

The rights of the child in Scotland

The Scotland Act 1998 (SA) provides that foreign affairs are reserved to the UK Parliament with the exceptions of observing and implementing international obligations and assisting UK ministers in the exercise of implementing international obligations.[61] Therefore, while UNCRC obligations in relation to reserved matters are outside legislative competence, obligations in relation to devolved matters are transferred to the Scottish ministers.[62] In practice, the Scottish government can implement the UNCRC in relation to devolved responsibilities.

Children and Young People (Scotland) Act 2014

The Children and Young People (Scotland) Act 2014 directly placed the UNCRC on statute for the first time.[63] Part 1 places duties on Scottish ministers to strengthen the approach taken to implement the UNCRC.[64] These duties have been criticised as being weak, placing little substantive obligation on government and providing no legal redress for children (Together, 2014).[65] No equivalent duties have been applied to public bodies, apart from a new reporting requirement designed to support the increased scrutiny of the public sector's approach to implementation.[66] Again, this has been criticised as a weak duty, which provides an obligation to publish a report rather than to take any action to further the UNCRC.[67] The duties on ministers commenced in June 2015, and

---

61 SA 1998, Sch.5 Pt 1 para 7(2).

62 SA 1998, s.53.

63 Available from URL: www.legislation.gov.uk/asp/2014/8/contents/enacted (accessed 16 February 2018).

64 2014 Act, Pt 1, s.1.

65 The Law Society of Scotland and Faculty of Advocates written evidence in relation to the Children and Young People (Scotland) Bill is available from URL: www.parliament. scot/S4_EducationandCultureCommittee/Children%20and%20Young%20People%20 (Scotland)%20Bill/FacultyofAdvocates.pdf (accessed 12 March 2018).

66 2014 Act, Pt 1, s.2.

67 Tisdall, E. K. M. (2015) 'Children's rights and children's well-being: Equivalent policy concepts?', Journal of Social Policy, Vol. 44, No. 4, p. 7.

the duties on public bodies became applicable in April 2017. It has been recognised that, despite being legally weak, the duties offer a significant opportunity to embed the UNCRC into the delivery of public services (Together, 2016). It will take many years until a full assessment of the impact of the 2014 Act can be made.

The Scottish picture
The patchwork of legal protections for children and young people's rights, both at a UK and Scottish level, has resulted in contradictions and conflicts in policy. In some cases, children's welfare eclipses parents' rights; in others, such as education, parents' considerations dominate.[68] There is also no consistent overview of how the interests of family members are managed across the generations, particularly in terms of allocating finite resources.[69]

In 2015, the Children's Commissioner highlighted five key concerns for children's rights in Scotland, as part of written evidence to the UK Joint Committee for Human Rights,[70] in advance of the UK's review of progress by the UNCRC.[71] These concerns included firstly legal protection rights under UNCRC,[72] and secondly problems with engagement and participation, in particular that the views of Scotland's most marginalised children and young people are not routinely heard or considered.[73] Thirdly, the Commissioner identified the impact of

---

68 For example, while the right to withdraw children from religious observance and instruction in schools is available to parents through Education (Scotland) Act 1980 s.9., no independent right of withdrawal is available to pupils. See: Cumper, P. and Mawhinney, A. (2015) 'Collective worship and religious observance in schools: An evaluation of law and policy in the UK' (online). Available from URL: http://bit.ly/2eF9Raz (accessed 16 February 2018).

69 Available from URL: www.jrf.org.uk/report/human-rights-obligations-and-policy-supporting-children-and-families (accessed 16 February 2018).

70 Available from URL: www.parliament.uk/business/committees/committees-a-z/joint-select/human-rights-committee (accessed 16 February 2018).

71 Available from URL: www.ohchr.org/EN/HRBodies/CRC/Pages/CRCIndex.aspx (accessed 16 February 2018).

72 Particularly the fact that some of Scotland's current legislation and policies breach the convention. These include:
- widespread use of non-statutory stop and search on children and young people;
- low age of criminal responsibility;
- the defence of 'justifiable assault' of a child;
- the unequal and discriminatory use of eligibility criteria for service provision.

73 The Commissioner specifically identified those who are very young, are gypsy/travellers, are black or minority ethnic and those have a disability.

austerity and child poverty, noting that austerity measures and welfare reform continue to have a disproportionate effect on children and young people: 'budget decisions do not generally take human rights into account and a combination of welfare reform measures are thought to risk increasing poverty' (SHRC, 2013). Poor access to mental health services was the fourth key issue, noting long waiting times, insufficient numbers of trained staff and treatment in inappropriate settings. The lack of specialist facilities in Scotland was highlighted, with recognition that this sometimes results in children being treated in adult wards or sent to England for treatment. The final key area was lack of equal protection: just like adults, children and young people have the right to respect for their human dignity and physical integrity.

These concerns were also highlighted by NGOs,[74] children and young people,[75] the SHRC[76] and the Children's Commissioner[77] during the UK's review by the CRC. This resulted in widespread recommendations from the CRC (echoing those made by other international human rights bodies) to address these issues.[78]

For example, the CRC called for the principles and provisions of the UNCRC to be made directly applicable and justiciable in domestic law. It also repeated calls for an increase in the age of criminal responsibility and for all corporal punishment within families to be outlawed. In response, the Scottish government has confirmed it will undertake an audit on the implementation of the UNCRC in Scotland, including the option of full incorporation into domestic law, raise the age of criminal responsibility from eight to twelve years old[79] and support a bill to

---

74 Available from URL: http://togetherscotland.org.uk/resources-and-networks/state-of-childrens-rights-reports (accessed 16 February 2018).

75 Available from URL: www.cypcs.org.uk/ufiles/UN-Taskforce-Visit-report.pdf (accessed 16 February 2018).

76 Available from URL: http://tbinternet.ohchr.org/_layouts/treatybodyexternal/Download.aspx?symbolno=INT%2fCRC%2fIFN%2fGBR%2f23800&Lang=en (accessed 16 February 2018).

77 Available from URL: http://tbinternet.ohchr.org/_layouts/treatybodyexternal/Download.aspx?symbolno=INT%2fCRC%2fIFN%2fGBR%2f21049&Lang=en (accessed 16 February 2018).

78 Available from URL: http://tbinternet.ohchr.org/_layouts/treatybodyexternal/Download.aspx?symbolno=CRC%2fC%2fGBR%2fCO%2f5&Lang=en (accessed 16 February 2018).

79 Available from URL: www.gov.scot/Publications/2017/09/8468/downloads (accessed 16 February 2018).

remove the defence of 'justifiable assault' in Scottish law.[80] Further-more, the Scottish Cabinet held its first official meeting with children and young people in March 2016, and has committed to make this an annual event to ensure their voices are taken into account in high-level decision-making.[81] While, as previously stated, there is a limited inter-pretive function of the UNCRC in the absence of incorporation, these positive steps demonstrate how international human rights conven-tions can influence the direction of travel.

Practice Example: ROSHNI[82]

Roshni is a Glasgow-based charity that works with minority ethnic com-munities across Scotland to address issues that affect them. The SAFE Project aims to raise awareness of child abuse and promote child protec-tion practices within minority ethnic communities (participation). The project uses the UNCRC as a framework to increase awareness and understanding of children's rights (accountability). SAFE provides community outreach programmes designed for children and young people. The programmes are delivered in culturally- and faith-sensitive workshops, which cover topics including healthy and unhealthy relationships, rights, child abuse and online safety (non-discrimination). These workshops increase aware-ness and understanding of abuse in all its forms and the ability to recognise signs of abuse. They provide children and young people with the means to take measures to prevent abuse and to access relevant support services (empowerment). They also ensure that children know they can access legal support to exercise their rights.

A person-centred approach and a HRBA draw from the same root-stock – respecting, protecting and promoting the inherent dignity of the individual. This should form the solid underpinning of health and social care and legal policy and practice. The next example is not, on the face of it, a human rights case; however, it fulfils the criteria for person-centred practice and a HRBA.

---

80 In October 2017, Scottish Government Ministers said that they will ensure that a Bill brought forward by Green MSP John Finnie would become law. The legislation will remove the defence of 'justifiable assault' in Scottish law, which allows parents to use physical punishment to admonish a child. Available from URL: www.independent.co.uk/news/uk/home-news/scotland-smacking-ban-corporal-punishment-parents-children-john-finnie-bill-justifiable-assault-a8009111.html (accessed 16 February 2018).

81 Available from URL: www.gov.scot/Topics/People/Young-People/families/youth-work-participation (accessed 16 February 2018).

82 Available from URL: www.scottishhumanrights.com/media/1408/shrc_case_studies_report.pdf (accessed 16 February 2018).

Legal Case example: Re A: Letter to a Young Person[83]

This was a private law case, heard by Mr Justice Peter Jackson, concerning the future of a fourteen-year-old boy who, for the purposes of the case, was called Sam.

Sam lived with his mother and stepfather and saw his father regularly. The father wanted to move to an identified Scandinavian country; Sam had advised that he wanted to go with him. The situation was emotive and contentious. A further issue was whether Sam should give evidence; there were competing views. Mr Justice Jackson resolved that Sam should give evidence at the beginning of the hearing but should not be questioned directly by either parent. Instead, each of them prepared five questions which, after his solicitor had asked him five introductory questions, Mr Justice Jackson put to Sam himself. Sam's evidence took less than half an hour after which he left the court and went on a school trip for the rest of the week, which was what he wanted.[84]

Unusually, Mr Justice Jackson gave his judgement in the form of a letter to Sam. The letter was written in clear, age-appropriate language but did not avert from the very difficult issues of family dynamics that were at the core of the judgement. Mr Justice Jackson decided it was in Sam's best interest to remain living in the UK with his mother and stepfather and to continue to have contact with his father, a decision that, on the face of it, did not accord with Sam's expressed wishes. It is, however, a wonderful example of balanced judgement and humanity, and one that should be read as an exemplar of a person-centred and human rights based approach.

Mr Justice Jackson ensured Sam's meaningful participation in the proceedings. The method of delivering the judgement ensured accountability to Sam, first and foremost. The fairness and balance illustrated in the letter evidences a non-discriminatory approach to parental roles and equally to a child's right to be heard and respected. Mr Justice Jackson empowered Sam by clearly setting out both the legal and evidential basis for the judgement that would so directly affect his life.

A HRBA can also inform the development of policy and practice without recourse to the court, as illustrated in the next example.

Practice and Policy Example: Kinship Care

Thousands of children in Scotland live full-time with their grandparents, aunts, uncles and family friends because their parents are unable to care for

83 A (Letter to a Young Person), Re (Rev 1) [2017] EWFC 48 (26 July 2017).
84 ibid., para 2.

them. Sometimes, this is a formal arrangement made with the involvement and support of local authorities and courts,[85] and, sometimes, it is informal and arranged within the family.[86] The EHRC[87] identified serious human rights concerns in relation to the financial support provided by some local authorities to looked-after children in kinship care. They were particularly concerned with arrangements in four councils where a lower level of kinship allowance and the inability to claim state benefits resulted in looked-after children in kinship care receiving c.60–70% less money per week than those in foster care.[88] In a report shared with the Scottish Government and Coalition of Scottish Local Authorities (COSLA), the EHRC expressed concern that the actions of these councils may be in violation of the ECHR Article 14 in conjunction with Article 8 and Article 1 of Protocol 1. Section 6 of the Human Rights Act 1998 makes it unlawful for a public authority to act in a way which is incompatible with a Convention right.

The Scottish government and COSLA responded positively to the report, agreeing both interim and longer-term plans to address the issues raised. The outcome of the EHRC's work on kinship allowances represents considerable progress in addressing issues facing kinship families in Scotland. Presenting robust evidence of potential human rights violations for the attention of lawyers and policymakers realised significant additional funding and a change in policy. This was, of course, reinforced by the EHRC's legal powers to challenge such violations.

Adopting a HRBA in this scenario may have avoided a situation where compliance is sought under threat of judicial review. Ensuring the participation of kinship carers at a strategic level, both locally and nationally, may have provided an appropriate forum for such anomalies to be raised and resolved. Transparency and accountability may

---

85 There are 4,181 looked-after children in Scotland who are living with family or friends (Scottish Government, 2015, *Education Outcomes for Scotland's Looked After Children 2013/14*, Edinburgh: Scottish Government, table 1.1, p. 7).

86 Citizens Advice Scotland (2014) 'In the family way: Five years of caring for Kinship Carers in Scotland' (online). Available from URL: www.cas.org.uk/system/files/publications/kinship%20care.pdf (accessed 16 February 2018).

87 The EHRC was set up under the Equality Act 2006 to challenge discrimination and to protect and promote human rights in Britain. Part of its role is to identify and tackle areas where there is still discrimination or where human rights are not being respected. The Commission has a range of enforcement and strategic litigation powers including inquiries, investigations, unlawful act notices and binding agreements. Its strategic litigation powers include taking judicial review proceedings in its own-name and intervening in legal cases taken by others.

88 Available from URL: www.equalityhumanrights.com/en/legal-work-scotland/legal-work-scotland/scottish-legal-articles/human-rights-children-kinship-care (accessed 16 February 2018).

enable comparative analysis, which in turn would highlight any inequities. Instead of relying on data being acquired through Freedom of Information requests, open sharing of data would allow for routine checks that a non-discriminatory approach was being adopted. This transparency would empower not only kinship carers but also practitioners and academics, thereby enabling greater oversight of this area of practice, which, in turn, is more likely to ensure the ongoing legality of the position adopted.

Conclusion

The UNCRC is the most widely ratified international human rights treaty in the world and has changed the way children are viewed and treated in international legal terms. The Convention sets out the status of children and young people as human beings with their own distinct set of rights, rather than as possessions of their parents or passive objects of care and charity. The rights contained in the fifty-four articles of the UNCRC are universal, interdependent and interrelated, and they cover all aspects of children's and young people's lives. If one right is not fulfilled, it can impact on other rights. As highlighted by the Children's Commissioner, a failure to tackle child poverty can, for example, impact on a child's mental health.

While there has been an increasing momentum to progress the human rights of children and young people in Scotland, their UNCRC rights are still not adequately protected in UK or Scots law. The UNCRC has gained a stronger legal basis through the Children and Young People (Scotland) Act 2014, but national and local government is under no obligation to act compatibly with its provisions. As such, children and young people are still not empowered to hold government to account in terms of its obligations under the UNCRC in the courts. Furthermore, parents are not always empowered with the necessary level of support they need to guarantee and promote the rights of their children.

Clearly, it is possible to adopt a HRBA, working within the current legal frameworks, to advance the rights of children and young people in Scotland and beyond. The implementation of the 2014 Act provides an opportunity to explore how non-legislative measures, such as child rights impact assessments, participation of children in decision-making and complaints mechanisms for children, can help to progress UNCRC implementation.

This includes the opportunity to support public bodies to embed a rights-based approach into their work with and for children and young people as part of their new duties under the 2014 Act.

Furthermore, accountability and public scrutiny through the UNCRC reporting process is also driving legislative and policy change. This has been evidenced through the Scottish government's recent commitment to raise the age of criminal responsibility and to give children equal protection from assault. Such progress tends to be approached in a piecemeal fashion and does not allow for the indivisible and interdependent nature of the rights enshrined in the UNCRC. To date, it has proved less effective in relation to progressing economic, social and cultural rights.

The Roshni case study highlights the importance of ensuring children and young people are aware of their rights. The greater the awareness of rights, the higher the likelihood of being able to empower children and young people to secure respect for them. The kinship care case study demonstrates the added weight that justiciable rights in domestic law can bring to achieving change, even without the need to resort to the courts. While case law helps to improve the implementation of children's rights, it is a slow, limited process which can be difficult for children to access and progress. As such, the courts are often not the ideal environment for children and young people to enforce their rights (although it should be an avenue available when all other options have failed).

In the absence of the incorporation of the UNCRC into domestic law in Scotland, further legislative progress relies on political will alone. However, even within the existing legislative environment, there is still great potential to bring about a culture change that will improve children and young people's lived experience of their rights. As the case studies in this chapter illustrate, the PANEL principles provide a powerful navigational tool with which to chart the required culture change. They also empower policymakers and practitioners to embed a HRBA into their work with children and young people.

CHAPTER 3

The Rights of Women

The principle of shared power and responsibility should be established between women and men at home, in the workplace and in the wider national and international communities. Equality between women and men is a matter of human rights and a condition for social justice and is also a necessary and fundamental prerequisite for equality, development and peace (United Nations, 1995).

Introduction

Human rights are 'universal'; however, there is a recognisable deficit between the aspirational rhetoric and lived reality of women worldwide. There is a continuing disparity between the life chances of girl children and their male counterparts. This is reflected in the experience of women in Scotland. Women are the majority of unpaid carers, lone parents, recipients of social security, low-paid workers, and survivors of domestic abuse and sexual violence in Scotland (Engender, 2017). This chapter will explore the systemic biases that continue to inhibit the life chances of girls and women. The gender-neutral approach adopted in early human rights instruments with the focus on the public/private dichotomy will be reviewed alongside the development of gender-specific conventions and the influence this has had on developing jurisprudence. Consideration will be given to specific legal cases and practice examples that illustrate the benefits of a HRBA. It is notable that very few legal cases and practice examples appear to be readily identifiable in terms of human rights, women and social care. This is, in and of itself, remarkable as women constitute the majority of social care clients. In 2015, 62% of social care at home clients and 69% of long-stay care home residents were female.[1] Women also make up the vast majority of the paid work-force; as in healthcare, about 80% of all jobs in adult social care are done by women; the proportion in direct care and support-providing jobs is higher, at 85–95%.[2] Women make up 59% of the unpaid workforce.[3]

The absence of women specific human and rights and social care cases, has necessitated that the legal and practice cases used to illustrate a HRBA in this chapter have been drawn from wider afield. As before, the PANEL principles of participation, accountability, non-discrimination, empower-ment and legality will be used as a reflexive tool to illustrate the benefits of adopting a HRBA. Particular attention will be paid to the developing jurisprudence of the ECtHR in relation to domestic abuse and the role that human rights instruments have played in informing policy and practice. This key area of evolving jurisprudence is particularly pertinent to the issue of women's rights. Importantly, it reveals an increased awareness of States' requirement to protect the rights of women against the activities of private individuals, whether within the public or private (domestic) sphere.

Discrimination and violence against girls begins at the earliest stages of life and continues unabated throughout their lives. One of the chal-lenges when writing this chapter has been the issue of intersectionality. The recognition that, traditionally, the dominant conception of discrimination viewed 'subordination as disadvantage occurring along a single categori-cal axis' (Crenshaw, 1989, p. 140). Women, however, experience overlap-ping systems of oppression and discrimination not just based on gender but also on ethnicity, sexuality, disability, economic status and other axes. Failure to recognise this can obscure claims that cannot be understood because they result from discrete sources of discrimination (Crenshaw, 1989). Women's experiences are multilayered and multifaceted, all of which requires consideration when looking at the implications of human rights in the field of social care. There follows a brief and limited overview of some key demographics.

---

1   Social Care services refer to: home care; telecare/community alarm; housing support; direct payments; and meals services. ISD Scotland (n.d.) 'Social care survey: Care home census' (online). Available from URL: www.isdscotland.org/Health-Topics/Health-and-Social-Community-Care/Care-Homes/Census (accessed 16 February 2018).

2   The King's Fund, 'Time to think differently' (online). Available from URL: www.kingsfund.org.uk/projects/time-think-differently/trends-workforce-overview (accessed 16 February 2018).

3   Scottish Government (2015) 'Scotland's carers' (online). Available from URL: http://www.gov.scot/Publications/2015/03/1081 (accessed 16 February 2018).

Definition and demography

Scotland had an estimated population of 5.4 million in 2016,[4] 51% of whom were women and 49% were men. This proportion has not changed much since 1947.[5] The population of Scotland is projected to rise to 5.58 million in 2026 and to continue to rise to 5.69 million in 2041. Some 18% of the Scottish population was estimated to be sixty-five plus in 2016.[6] Between 2016 and 2041, the population of pensionable age is projected to rise from 1.05 million to 1.32 million, an increase of 25%.[7] Recent life-expectancy estimates for Scotland are for boys born in 2015 to live 76.9 years on average, 59.9 of these in a 'healthy' state. Girls born in 2015 would be expected to live 81.0 years on average, 62.3 of these years being 'healthy'.[8] Based on the projections available, the population of Scotland will be become older and more female, a change that health and social care service systems need to plan for.

Welfare reform has had a greater impact on women (IFS, 2011), with certain groups of women, including lone mothers, refugees, disabled women, unpaid carers and women experiencing domestic abuse, facing multiple and particularly extreme impacts as a result (Engender, 2015). In 2012, 30% of men and 35% of women in Scotland reported a limiting long-term condition or disability (Scottish Government, 2016a). In 2016, 2.2% of the population identified as lesbian, gay or bisexual (LGB), broken down as 1.2% identifying as gay or lesbian and 1.0% as bisexual. Women experience many overlapping layers of disadvantage, which needs to be recognised in order for their rights to be respected and protected.[9]

In terms of economic well-being, systemic issues mean women are twice as dependent on social security as men; are twice as likely to give up paid

4 Available from URL: www.nrscotland.gov.uk/files/statistics/high-level-summary/j11198/j1119804.htm (accessed 16 February 2018).
5 NRS mid-2016 population estimates Scotland.
6 Available from URL: www.nrscotland.gov.uk/files/statistics/high-level-summary/j11198/j1119802.htm (accessed 16 February 2018).
7 Available from URL: www.nrscotland.gov.uk/news/2017/scotlands-population-is-projected-to-increase-and-to-age (accessed 16 February 2018).
8 Available from URL: www.gov.scot/Topics/Statistics/Browse/Health/TrendLifeExpectancy (accessed 16 February 2018).
9 Women's Resource Centre (2010) *In All Our Colours: Lesbian, Bisexual and Trans Women's Services in the UK*, London: Women's Resource Centre. Available from URL: http://thewomensresourcecentre.org.uk/wp-content/uploads/IAOC.pdf (accessed 16 February 2018).

work to become unpaid carers; and are four times as likely to give up paid work to provide 'sandwich care' (Carers UK, 2012). Women are still concentrated in lower-paying occupations, with nearly two-thirds of women employed in twelve occupation groups, most of which are related to women's traditional roles in the family – caring, cashiering, catering, cleaning and clerical occupations, as well as teaching, health-associated professions (including nursing) and 'functional' manager posts (e.g. financial managers, marketing and sales managers and personnel managers) (Women and Work Commission, 2009). Other structural factors include the gender skills gap, particularly for older women, because there is less access to training in the lower-paid sectors, where more women than men tend to work (Women and Work Commission, 2009).[10] But most important is the fact that women remain primarily responsible for childcare. Some 92% of lone parents are women, and women make up 95% of lone parents on income support. Taking time out of the labour market, amassing less experience, limitations in respect of travel to work, and part-time working, all extract a severe wage penalty (Fredman, 2013). In 2015, the overall gender pay gap in Scotland stood at 14.8%, with women over-represented in informal, temporary and part-time work, and more likely to be paid below the living wage. Disabled women are less likely to be employed, and they experience a much higher pay gap than other women (SHRC, 2017).

Women's equal participation in public, political and cultural institutions is pivotal to the advancement of women more generally. Women are not equally represented in political and public life – an issue that requires concerted action to address. The UK continues to be run largely by men (Centre for Women and Democracy, 2015), with the top positions in public life within the political parties, government, public bodies, regional and local authorities, the judiciary, police, private and public sectors held by men (Cracknell, 2012). Making up more than half the Scottish population, women should be equally represented across the spectrum of civic life; women currently make up: 35% of MSPs, 25% of local councillors, 16% of council leaders, 17% of MEPs, 28% of public body chief executives, 26% of university principals, 23% of sheriffs, 7% of senior police officers, 0% of major newspaper editors, 19% of major museums and art galleries

---

10 See also 'Closing the gender skills gap: A national skills forum report on women, skills and productivity' (online). Available from URL: www.policyconnect.org.uk/apgse/research/closing-gender-skills-gap (accessed 12 March 2018).

directors, 14% of national sports bodies chief executives and 0% of CEOs of 'top' businesses (Engender, 2017, p. 6).

Women's inequality also finds expression in the level of violence women experience. According to a March 2014 EU-wide survey, violence against women is 'an extensive human rights abuse' across Europe, with one in three women reporting some form of physical or sexual abuse from the age of fifteen and 8% suffering abuse in the last twelve months (FRA, 2014).

The Scottish government has taken steps to address violence against women and has committed additional funding to ensure that victims will 'have the confidence to report crime'. In 2016/17, there were 58,810 incidents of domestic abuse recorded by the police in Scotland – an increase of 1% from 2015/16; 47% of incidents of domestic abuse recorded by the police in Scotland resulted in at least one crime or offence being committed.[11] It is estimated that 15.6% of women aged between sixteen and sixty-four years – that is one in six – have a long-standing health problem or disability. The biggest differences are found in terms of physical or sexual partner violence: 34% of women with a health problem or disability have experienced this during a relation-ship, compared with 19% of women who do not have a health problem or disability (FRA, 2014). EU law has advised that the UK and Scotland strengthen human rights protections, including for victims of violence (SHRC, 2017).

It has been suggested that 'the concept of human rights is one of the few moral visions ascribed internationally' (Bunch, 1992). Some academics posit that domestic abuse violates the fundamental tenets of this moral vision (Thomas and Beasley, 1993), clearly articulated in the preamble to the UN Declaration of Human Rights as 'the inherent dignity and of the equal and inalienable rights of all members of the human family'.[12] It has also been noted that, until relatively recently, domestic violence appeared to fall out with the scope of much human rights discourse. That scant ECtHR jurisprudence exists prior to 2007 appears to support this position. Traditionally, the home has been conceived of as a sanctuary. Research, however, appears to indicate that 'far from being a place of safety, the family can be [a] "cradle of violence" and that much of this violence

---

11 Available from URL: www.gov.scot/Topics/Statistics/Browse/Crime-Justice/
    TrendDomesticAbuse (accessed 16 February 2018).
12 Preamble to the Universal Declaration of Human Rights, signed 10 December 1948, UN
    Doc. A/810 at 71.

is directed at the female members of the family' (Connors, 1989, p. 14). Domestic violence is defined as:

> all acts of physical, sexual, psychological or economic violence that occur within the family or domestic unit or between former or current spouses or partners, whether or not the perpetrator shares or has shared the same residence with the victim.[13]

The following common characteristics emerge from international research: domestic violence is not unusual or an exception to normal family life; the vast majority of violence against women happens in the home; and domestic violence is endemic in all societies (Schuler, 1992, p. 1). Globally, domestic violence is the most common form of violence against women.[14] Socio-economic rights may be particularly important in relation to domestic violence, as the most pressing need for victims may be social support in the form of housing, emergency refuge accommodation and monetary assistance. The question worth considering is why domestic violence has not, until relatively recently, been framed as a human rights issues.

Historical development of human rights and the rights of women

It has been argued that, despite the Vienna Declaration of 1993 which stated that all human rights are 'universal, indivisible and interdependent and interrelated',[15] a hierarchy of rights exists, with civil and political rights given far greater priority while economic, social and cultural rights are relegated to the second bench. This could be considered a white Western, gendered approach to rights that particularly benefits an influential subset of society – white Western adult males (Johnstone, 2006).

It is also argued that the negative formulation of human rights law has curtailed opportunities for the development of human rights law in practice (Mowbray, 2005, p. 60). The counter argument is that,

---

13 Council of Europe, Convention on preventing and combatting violence against women and domestic violence (Istanbul Convention), Article 3b.

14 CPS, WRC and Unicef (2014) 'Empowered and safe" Economic strengthening for girls in emergencies' (online). Available from URL: www.womensrefugeecommission. org/component/zdocs/document/1151-empowered-andsafe?catid=247 (accessed 16 February 2018).

15 Article 5 of the Vienna Declaration, A/CONF.157/23, 12 July 1993.

increasingly, the positive responsibilities of States are being incorporated into international human rights law and practice: for example,
CEDAW requires governments to take positive measures to end legal,
social and economic gender inequality. Human rights law is developing
in such a way as to now more readily enter the private sphere. In addition, national courts may apply ordinary law in a manner that is protective of rights. This has been referred to as an indirect horizontal effect
or the interpretative obligation. As an example, McQuigg cites Section
3 of the UK's Human Rights Act 1998, which states that the courts
must interpret statutes in accordance with the rights contained in the
ECHR, so far as it is possible to do so. The principle of State responsibility has been developed, under which positive obligations can be placed
directly on the State to ensure that human rights standards are upheld
in situations involving only private individuals. This development has
profound implications for the State's approach to domestic violence.
One of the significant challenges is the issue of balancing rights when
conflicting interests exist (Mowbray, 2010).

International human rights law is, on the face of it, with the exception for obvious reasons of CEDAW (see below), presented as gender-
neutral. It has been argued that, although purportedly gender-neutral
in theory, in practice international human rights law 'interacts with
gender-biased domestic laws that separate women and men into different spheres of existence: private and public' (Charlesworth *et al.*, 1991,
p. 613). The public/private dichotomy is considered by many feminist
theorists to be 'a fundamental ordering principle of western culture'
(Patterson, 1990, p. 315). The roots of international human rights law
draw largely from Western political theory based upon the rights of
the individual to autonomy and freedom (Thomas and Beasley, 1993).
Strongly influenced by the long shadow of the atrocities experienced
during the Second World War, international human rights law developed to protect the individual from the worst vagaries of the State.

The exclusive focus on the behaviour of the State narrowed the focus
of international human rights law to that considered to be in the 'public
sphere'. This negative formulation of human rights created a public/
private dichotomy where human rights norms are upheld in the public
sphere, where the State is involved, but do not apply in the private or
domestic sphere. Charlesworth and Chinkin (2000, p. 33) suggest that

an 'important function of the (public/private) dichotomy in liberal jurisprudence is to demarcate areas appropriate for legal regulation from those that come within the sphere of individual autonomy'. The forms of human rights abuses that occur in the private sphere disproportionately affect women and include domestic violence, female genital mutilation, dowry killings and sati (McQuigg, 2011).

If human rights law is to challenge the public/private dichotomy, the 'absolute' right to be free from torture or inhuman and degrading treatment may prove to be a useful lens through which to challenge the issue of domestic violence. In most cases, this right is taken to apply only when the State itself is inflicting the prohibited treatment. The United Nations Convention against Torture states that activity must be 'inflicted by or at the instigation of or with the consent or acquiescence of a public official or other person acting in an official capacity'. Parallels have been drawn by feminist theorists between domestic violence and torture (Grdinic, 1999), with the former, until relatively recently, afforded no protection under human rights law. It has been argued that 'inclusion of domestic violence in norms against torture may well change the perception of domestic violence on both international and domestic levels' (Hopkins, 2001, p. 435).

Convention on the Elimination of All Form of Discrimination Against Women (CEDAW)[16]

CEDAW was adopted by the UN General Assembly in 1979. It is often described as an international bill of rights for women. Consisting of a preamble and thirty Articles, it defines what constitutes discrimination against women and sets an agenda for national action to end such discrimination. The Convention defines discrimination against women as:

> ... any distinction, exclusion or restriction made on the basis of sex which has the effect or purpose of impairing or nullifying the recognition, enjoyment or exercise by women, irrespective of their marital status, on a basis of equality of men and women, of human rights and fundamental freedoms in the political, economic, social, cultural, civil or any other field.[17]

---

16 CEDAW was adopted and opened for signature, ratification and accession by General Assembly resolution 34/180 of 18 December 1979, entry into force 3 September 1981, in accordance with Article 27(1).

17 ibid., Article 1.

The Convention goes beyond the concept of discrimination used in many national and international legal standards and norms. While such standards and norms prohibit discrimination on the grounds of sex and protect both men and women from treatment based on arbitrary, unfair and/or unjustifiable distinctions, the Convention focuses on discrimination against women, emphasising that women have suffered, and continue to suffer, from various forms of discrimination because they are women.[18] The Convention provides the basis for realising equality between women and men through ensuring women's equal access to, and equal opportunities in, political and public life. State parties agree to take all appropriate measures including legislation and temporary special measures, so that women can enjoy all their human rights and fundamental freedoms.[19]

The Convention is the only human rights treaty which affirms the reproductive rights of women and targets culture and tradition as influential forces shaping gender roles and family relations. Countries that have ratified or acceded to the Convention are legally bound to put its provisions into practice. They are also committed to submit national reports, at least every four years, on measures they have taken to comply with their treaty obligations. The UK signed CEDAW in July 1981 but it was not ratified until April 1986. A lack of interest in the substance of the Convention has marked the attitude of successive governments ever since. As previously stated, the UK has a dualist system of international law, meaning that treaties are not binding unless incorporated by legislation. Successive UK governments have consistently refused to incorporate CEDAW into domestic law (Fredman, 2013).

Oversight and monitoring
The CEDAW Committee is the body composed of independent experts charged with monitoring the implementation of CEDAW. States parties to the treaty are obliged to submit regular reports to the Committee on how Convention rights are being implemented. The Committee considers each State party report and addresses its concerns and recommendations to the State party in the form of concluding observations.

18 General recommendation No. 25, on CEDAW Article 4, para 1, on temporary special measures, para 5..
19 Available from URL: www.un.org/womenwatch/daw/cedaw (accessed 16 February 2018)

The Optional Protocol to the Convention on the Elimination of All Forms of Discrimination against Women is an international treaty which establishes complaint and inquiry mechanisms for the CEDAW. The UK acceded to the Protocol on 17 December 2004, and it entered into force on 17 March 2005. There are two principal aspects to the Optional Protocol, each of which is designed to enhance the effectiveness of the monitoring of State responsibilities. Firstly, the Committee is mandated to receive communications from individuals or groups of individuals submitting claims of violations of rights protected under the Convention. Secondly, the Committee can initiate inquiries into situations of grave or systematic violations of women's rights. Recognising the symbolic value of a State's recognition of the right to complain under the Optional Protocol, the actual impact in the UK has been negligible. On two occasions, the Committee has recognised violations and in doing so has also helped to emphasise the real importance of ensuring an effective response to serious and repeated instances of domestic violence and of protecting women against medical treatment without informed consent (Murdoch, 2008).[20]

The CEDAW Committee recognises that CEDAW is 'dynamic' and is required to respond to changing global circumstances. To address this, the Committee also formulates general recommendations and suggestions, which concern Articles or themes in the Convention (EHRC, 2014a).

For example, at the 1989 session, the Committee discussed the high incidence of violence against women, requesting information on this problem from all countries. In 1992, the Committee adopted General Recommendation No. 19 on violence against women, asking States parties to include in their periodic reports to the Committee statistical data on the incidence of violence against women, information on the provision of services for victims, and legislative and other measures taken to protect women against violence in their everyday lives, including against harassment at the workplace, abuse in the family and sexual violence.[21] General Recommendation No. 19 interprets the Convention as prohibiting violence against women in both public and private contexts. The recommendation states:

20 Available from URL: www.ohchr.org/EN/HRBodies/CEDAW/Pages/Introduction.aspx (accessed 16 February 2018).
21 Available from URL: www.ohchr.org/EN/HRBodies/CEDAW/Pages/ Recommendations.aspx (accessed 16 February 2018).

that discrimination under the Convention is not restricted to action by or on behalf of Governments ...Under general international law and specific human rights covenants, States may be responsible for private acts if they fail to act with due diligence to prevent violations of rights or to investigate and punish acts of violence, and for providing compensation.[22]

The CEDAW Committee recognises differences between women and men, both biologically and socially, and that, because of these differences, equal treatment under the law (formal or *de jure* equality) may not be enough to ensure women enjoy the same rights as men. Governments should seek to understand the root causes of inequalities between men and women, and to introduce laws, policies and public services that address them. This may mean treating women differently from men, to enable them to achieve the same results (EHRC, 2014a, p. 7). The Committee introduced General Recommendation No. 25, on CEDAW Article 4, para 1, on special measures.[23] The UK government introduced a Temporary Special Measure of women-only shortlists for political parties, to increase the number of women in Parliament. It can be used until 2030.

European Convention on Human Rights (ECHR) and the rights of women

Article 8(1) of the ECHR states that 'everyone has the right to respect for his private and family life'. However, Article 8(2) continues:

There shall be no interference by a public authority with the exercise of this right except such as in accordance with the law and is necessary in a democratic society in the interest of national security, public safety or the economic well-being of a country, for the prevention of disorder or crime, for the

---

22 UN Doc A/47/38 (1992), para 9.
23 General recommendation No. 25, on CEDAW Article 4, para 1, on temporary special measures. Para 12: 'Certain groups of women, in addition to suffering from discrimination directed against them as women, may also suffer from multiple forms of discrimination based on additional grounds such as race, ethnic or religious identity, disability, age, class, caste or other factors. Such discrimination may affect these groups of women primarily, or to a different degree or in different ways than men. States parties may need to take specific temporary special measures to eliminate such multiple forms of discrimination against women and its compounded negative impact on them'.

protection of health or morals, or for the protection of the rights and freedoms of others (Rainey *et al.*, 2014).

In relation to the issue of domestic violence, the rights of the victim may come into conflict with the right of an alleged perpetrator to a fair trial. It has been suggested that, if the balance between conflicting rights is not considered carefully, there is a danger that the human rights movement may find itself 'in the uncomfortable position of legitimating more injustice than it eliminates' (Kennedy, 2004). To consider this further, it is necessary to look at the role of the ECtHR.

In accordance with the underpinning principle of the ECHR as a living instrument, the jurisprudence of the ECtHR continues to evolve. The ECtHR has placed positive obligations upon states to intervene in situations where an individual's rights have been violated by another private entity. In respect of domestic violence, the ECtHR has transcended the public/private dichotomy that has constrained the scope of human rights law since its inception:

> domestic violence takes place between private individuals; therefore, in order for the European Convention on Human Rights to be used in relation to this issue, the doctrine of positive obligations must be engaged (McQuigg, 2011, p. 26).

The ECtHR appears to have drawn this principle from three areas. Firstly, Article 1 of the Convention requires States to safeguard rights to everyone within their jurisdiction, by implication requiring States to take positive steps to ensure citizens freely enjoy their fundamental rights. Secondly, recognising that rights are practical and effective and not merely theoretical requires that the social context within which rights are exercised is considered; therefore: 'passive non-interference by governmental authorities with persons' Convention rights is not sufficient to ensure that many of those rights are fully and effectively respected' (Mowbray, 2004, p. 221). Thirdly, Article 13 provides for another positive obligation when requiring States to provide effective remedies for violations of rights. This is a contested development open to criticism of judge-led activity, exceeding the intended scope of the Conventions. The ECtHR has balanced this challenge by operating a wide margin of appreciation when considering States positive obligations.

Osman v. United Kingdom is a significant and contentious ECtHR case that highlights the complexities of the court's approach to the State's positive obligations. The applicant's husband was killed by her son's former teacher and her son was seriously wounded. Before the incident, the teacher had previously threatened the applicant and the family. The applicant complained of the failure of authorities to protect the right to life of her husband from the threat posed by the teacher. The ECtHR did not find a violation of Article 2 of the ECHR on the basis that the evidence did not show that the police knew or ought to have known that the lives of the Osman family were at real and immediate risk. The court noted that the first sentence of Article 2(1) enjoins the State not only to refrain from the intentional and unlawful taking of life, but also to take appropriate steps to safeguard the lives of those within its jurisdiction. It may also imply in certain well-defined circumstances that there is a positive obligation on the authorities to take preventative operational measures to protect an individual whose life is at risk from the criminal acts of another individual.[24]

As previously stated, very little ECtHR jurisprudence existed in relation to domestic violence prior to 2007. Several key cases highlight the evolving nature of case law in this area in the intervening period. *Kontrova v. Slovakia*[25] is a case involving domestic violence where the applicant's husband killed himself and their two children. In this instance, the court found a violation of the Convention in a situation involving domestic violence. The breach was, however, found in relation to the right to life of the children, the abuse experienced by the applicant was not meaningfully addressed. In *Bavacqua and S v. Bulgaria*,[26] the applicant brought the case under Articles 3 and 8 of the Convention on the basis that authorities had failed to protect her and her son from violence at the hands of her husband. Finding there had been a violation, the court stated: 'the authorities' view that no assistance was due as the dispute concerned a "private matter" was incompatible with their positive obligations to secure the enjoyment of the applicants' Article 8 rights'.[27] The importance of this case is the finding on the basis of actual abuse experienced by a victim of domestic violence at

24 *Osman v. United Kingdom* (App. No. 23452/94) (1998) EHRR 249.

25 *Kontrova v. Slovakia* (App. No. 7510/04) (2006) EHR.

26 *Bavacqua and S v. Bulgaria* (App. No. 71127/01) (2008) EHRR 433.

27 ibid., para 83.

the hands of an individual and within a private domestic sphere. The *Opuz v. Turkey*[28] case was progressed based on a violation of Articles 2, 3 and 14. The applicant and her mother had experienced domestic violence at the hands of her husband, eventually resulting in the death of her mother. The court concluded that there had been a violation of Articles 2 and 3. Regarding Article 14, the court found that, in line with established international practice, the State's failure to protect women against domestic violence breached women's right to equal protection of the law. In the case of *Eremia and Others v. Moldova*[29] ECtHR took a further step towards recognising the discriminatory aspect of domestic violence against women, along with confirming the possibility of characterising domestic violence as inhuman treatment within the meaning of ECHR Article 3.

It is clear from the jurisprudence that domestic violence constitutes a clear violation of Articles 2, 3, 8 and 14 of the ECHR. The State has positive obligations, if narrowly defined, to ensure that the criminal and civil justice systems are sufficiently effective in response to issues that arise from domestic violence. The concept of State responsibility has gone some way to breach the private/public dichotomy and the ECtHR has shown a willingness to adjudicate on matters in the private sphere, even when the rights of an individual are infringed by another individual. Human rights law has a significant role to play in offering women who experience domestic violence the opportunity for protection and redress. One should not underestimate the myriad hurdles facing disempowered women seeking legal redress for domestic violence: accessing legal aid, overcoming cultural barriers and surmounting social and economic constraints to name a few. That said, the application of positive State obligations illustrated in the evolving ECtHR jurisprudence offers a glimmer of hope that international human rights law can play its part.

UK legislation

The ECHR is incorporated in the UK through the HRA; however, the UK government has consistently resisted incorporation of CEDAW and does not regard it as normative, in the sense of shaping policy or

---

28 *Opuz v. Turkey* (App. No. 33401/02) (2009) EHRR.
29 *Eremia and Others v. Moldova* (App. No. 3564/11) (2013) EHRR.

providing direction (Fredman, 2013). The law in the UK cannot move ahead of the legislature's willingness to develop. Given the constitutional make-up of the UK and sovereign role of Parliament, any attempt by the judiciary to strong-arm human rights based developments may result in legal procedural compliance with no intention to implement the spirit of human rights standards – an approach that may, in time, be self-defeating. The Equality Act 2010 created the Public Sector Equality Duty, which requires public sector organisations to have due regard to the need to:

- eliminate discrimination, harassment and victimisation and other prohibited conduct;
- advance equality of opportunity between persons who share a relevant protected characteristic such as race, gender or age, and persons who do not share it;
- foster good relations between persons who share a relevant protected characteristic and persons who do not share it.

The specific duties in Scotland require Scottish ministers to identify Scotland-wide equality priorities, and report on progress to the Scottish Parliament. Scottish public authorities are required to publish pay-gap information, and statements on equal pay. Despite the limitations of the impact of CEDAW, the evolving jurisprudence of the ECtHR appears to be informing decisions relating to human rights and equality for women – an approach that can be built upon.

Practical examples and case studies

The first legal case provides an excellent illustration of the inherent gender bias contained within purportedly gender-neutral policy and practice.

Legal Case: HA, R (on the Application of) v. London Borough of Ealing [2015][30]

In the case of *HA, R (on the Application of) v. London Borough of Ealing* [2015], the applicant was a victim of domestic violence who left her former family home with her children to escape the violence. She was denied the right to apply for housing by Ealing Council based on a blanket five-year residency requirement. The High Court found that the residency criteria, by not permitting the exception of women fleeing domestic violence and in the

---

30 *HA, R (On the Application Of) v. London Borough of Ealing,* Court of Appeal – Administrative Court [2015] EWHC 2375 (Admin)

absence of reasonable justification, was contrary to Article 14 of the ECHR (anti-discrimination). Echoes of the findings of *Opuz v. Turkey*[31] may be seen to resonate through this judgement.

Had the PANEL principles been applied as an assurance that a HRBA was being adopted, the discriminatory aspects of the policy may have been highlighted and the legality of the actions addressed before being required by the court.

As highlighted earlier, women are disproportionately represented in the field of social care, as citizens who use services, as family members and unpaid carers and as paid employees. Women experience overlapping layers of oppression and discrimination not just based on gender but also on ethnicity, sexuality, disability, economic status and other axes as illustrated in the following case examples.

Legal case: R (on the application of Bernard) v. Enfield LBC [2002][32]

Mr and Mrs Bernard and their six children lived in a home that was not suitable for their needs. Mrs Bernard was disabled and could access only one room in the house and had no access to the first floor where the bathroom and bedrooms were situated. This was a significant issue as she was incontinent. Although their local social services department recommended that the family be provided with specially adapted accommodation, the family heard nothing for well over a year. When their case came before a court, the judge held that the local authority had a positive obligation to enable the family to lead as normal a family life as possible and that they had not done this – in breach of Article 8 (the right to respect for family life).

Applying the PANEL principles to this situation the family's participation in the process and the accountability of social services to them on a regular basis might not necessarily have resolved the housing situation any sooner, if suitable accommodation were not available. It might, however, have enabled different discussions to take place to ameliorate the worst impacts of this untenable situation on the family in the interim. This shift of emphasis might have changed the dynamic from one in which the family were cast as passive recipients awaiting a resolution out of their control, to one where they were empowered and actively engaged in finding a range of temporary and longer-term

---

31 *supra* n. 28.
32 *Bernard v. London Borough of Enfield* [2002] EWHC 2282 (Admin).

solutions. A non-discriminatory approach may also have placed a greater focus on preservation of human dignity.[33] It is noteworthy that action was not taken under Article 3 (inhuman or degrading treatment or punishment). Reviewing the proposed course of action through the prism of the PANEL principles might have highlighted the significant legal risks that the local authority was taking in relation to its human rights obligations before these were highlighted by the court.

The final legal case example detailed below does not focus on the rights of women per se. As previously stated within this chapter, very few examples of legal cases based on the human rights and social care specific to women exist. The following legal case, while not being based on gender, usefully illustrates the importance of developing a HRBA, particularly in times of economic austerity and tightening budgets.

Gunter v. South-West Staffordshire PCT 2005[34]

A disabled woman who required twenty-four-hour care wanted to be supported to remain living with her family, facilitated by an extensive care package. Her local Primary Care Trust (PCT) wanted to place her in residential care due to the perceived high cost of home-based support. Concerns were also expressed about availability of support in the event of a crisis. The High Court found that the PCT had not properly considered the impact of their decision on her family life. They had not taken account of her improved quality of life at home, nor her expressed wish to remain at home. The PCT was, therefore, told to remake their decision, taking her right to respect for her family life (Article 8) into account.

Using a person-centred approach guided by the PANEL principles, the starting point for practitioners in this case would have been the full and meaningful participation of the focus person in the planning of their future support arrangement. Transparent and accountable processes would have assured the focus person that their expressed will and preferences were central to the plan. Adopting this approach would have afforded the opportunity to make any reasonable adjustments and would have ensured that

---

33 The International Covenant on Economic, Social and Cultural Rights (ICESCR) is a UN treaty that focuses on rights that are crucial to enable people to live with dignity. It covers areas such as working conditions, social security, adequate food, housing, health and education.

34 *Rachel Gunter (by her litigation friend, Edwin Gunter) v. South Western Staffordshire Primary Care Trust* [2005] EWHC 1894 (Admin).

a non-discriminatory assessment and planning process was being undertaken. This would have resulted in a more empowering process for both the focus person and those in her wider support network. It would also have been more likely to ensure the legality of the approach adopted by frontline practitioners and, ultimately, the funding authority.

Conclusion

International human rights are universal and as such apply to all regardless of gender, ethnicity, sexuality, disability and economic status. Women's experiences of discrimination and disadvantage are multilayered and, historically, 'abuses, exclusions and constraints that are more typical of women's lives are neither recognised nor protected by mainstream human rights instruments' (van Leeuwen, 2009, p. 9). In relation to the ECHR, primacy has been afforded to civil and political rights based on a legacy of the negative framing of rights. Following the doctrine of the 'living instrument', ECtHR jurisprudence has evolved over time and, as has been evidenced in this chapter, there appears to be a growing recognition that public/private dichotomy fails to protect women equally.

Social care is an area of societal activity where women feature predominantly as citizens who use services, as informal carers or as employees working in the field, and women often occupy multiple roles at the same time. Proactively adopting the PANEL principles as a core aspect engagement would ensure that social care made a meaningful contribution towards the realisation of the human rights of women – and more so during times of austerity, when it is recognised that budget reductions that impact on social care disproportionately affect women. Adopting a HRBA may provide policymakers, practitioners and women who use services with a bulwark against the worst excesses of budget-driven social care reform. The PANEL principles offer policymakers and practitioners a tool with which to balance the human rights of women against the pressing demands of the bottom line on a balance sheet.

CHAPTER 4

The Rights of Disabled People

> Human rights consequently involve more than what is actually covered by legislation. Laws can regulate certain conditions for disabled people but they cannot completely affect the conditions of their existence and their opportunity for personal development – the realisation of human rights needs to come into existence in the full cultural and human context (Nirje, 1985, p. 65).

Introduction

Despite the universality of human rights, disabled people experience greater levels of discrimination and prejudice and require specific measures of protection to ensure their rights are upheld. More than half of the disabled people who took part in a poll reported having experienced hostility, aggression or violence from a stranger because of their condition or impairment (Scope, 2011). The right of disabled people to be free from exploitation, violence and abuse is guaranteed in Article 16 of the UN Convention on the Rights of Persons with Disabilities (CRPD).[1] This includes explicit obligations to take effective steps to prevent exploitation, violence and abuse, to act to protect disabled people and to remedy its effects.[2] Article 16(5) further requires that:

> States Parties shall put in place effective legislation and policies, including women and child focused legislation and policies, to ensure that instances of exploitation, violence and abuse against persons with disabilities are identified, investigated and where appropriate, prosecuted.

---

1 https://www.un.org/development/desa/disabilities/convention-on-the-rights-of-persons-with-disabilities.html (accessed 12 March 2018).
2 CRPD Article 16(2).

The EHRC (2011) raised concern that harassment of disabled people remains widespread in Scotland, noting a failure on the part of public bodies to take appropriate action to address the issue. The tone of public discourse around the issue of welfare reform has been highlighted as a contributory factor (SCOPE, 2011). This may be regarded as an issue of power, that 'while one social group have the power to represent, through whatever media, the reality of those perceived as different, there is always a danger that the "other" will be seen as not quite human (Morris, 2001, p. 6).

In the wake of the global economic downturn in 2008, the UK government launched a major policy of reform of the welfare system, aimed at reducing the fiscal deficit and achieving a surplus in its balance of payments by 2020 (Audit Scotland, 2014). In terms of general provision to meet their essential needs, people with disabilities and their families are suffering more than any other section of society from current financial constraints (Law Society of Scotland, 2012, p. 3). A 2016 inquiry report by the UN Committee on the Rights of Persons with Disabilities under Article 6 of the Optional Protocol raised significant concerns in relation to the UK's adherence to human rights obligations.[3] The report noted that amendments to welfare and social care represent a major reform of the social policy system and that austerity measures are the underlying reason for it (Goodley et al., 2014).[4] It also highlighted concerns expressed by NHRI (EHRC, 2014b), local authorities (LGA, 2013) and the UK Parliament (House of Lords, House of Commons Joint Committee on Human Rights, 2011) about the potentially discriminatory effects of welfare measures on people with disabilities. The Scottish government undertook impact assessments, which identified impacts in groups with protected characteristics, including people with disabilities (Scottish Government, 2014a;[5] Scottish Government, 2014b)[6] Critically, one report highlighted that, as a consequence of these actions, the deinstitutionalisation process had been adversely affected (Scottish Government, 2014a, p. 17). The Committee

---

3 With a focus on Article 19: Living independently and living in the community; Article 27: Work and employment; and Article 28: Adequate standard of living and social protection.

4 Available from URL: www.ohchr.org/Documents/HRBodies/CRPD/ CRPD.C.15.R.2.Rev.1-ENG.doc (accessed 16 February 2018).

5 Available from URL: www.gov.scot/Resource/0045/00457564.pdf (accessed 16 February 2018).

6 Available from URL: www.gov.scot/Resource/0046/00463006.pdf (accessed 16 February 2018).

on the Rights of Persons with Disabilities' concluding observations on the first periodic review in 2017 made headlines when the Chair of the panel spoke of the implications of welfare reform as a 'human catastrophe' for disabled people.[7]

It is within this societal context that this chapter considers the human rights of disabled people in relation to social care, looking both at the ECHR and the CRPD. The PANEL principles of participation, accountability, non-discrimination, empowerment and legality, detailed in Chapter 1, will be used as a lens with which to consider particularly interesting or significant case law and practice examples. While undertaking research for this book, the lack of social care related judicial reviews in Scotland became apparent. There is also a distinct absence of case law relating to disabled people and, more specifically, those referring to human rights. Highlighting this phenomenon is not to suggest that litigation is the most appropriate way to resolve differences. The lack of judicial oversight and, ultimately, case law is notable – more so considering significant policy developments such as the introduction of SDS, which have the potential to expose areas of contention, particularly when implemented in an era of budget cuts. The judicial silence is not necessarily benign, and, while further consideration of this issue is beyond the scope of this chapter, it is a subject worthy of further investigation.

This chapter focuses on the contentious issue of legal and mental capacity and the implications for disabled people. The impact of capacity-based decision-making on the human rights of people with learning disabilities will be afforded particular attention. Before embarking on this, consideration will be given to the importance of language in this field, followed by a brief overview of the development of the disability movement in the UK in the context of social care.

Language – definition

Use of language is significant when framing the issue of human rights, disability and social care. Choice of words can project a philosophical standpoint reflective of the continuing tension between the medical and social model of disability; a brief overview of these approaches

---

7   Available from URL: http://www.independent.co.uk/news/uk/politics/government-spending-cuts-human-catastrophe-un-committee-rights-persons-with-disabilities-disabled-a7911556.html (accessed 16 February 2018).

is provided later in this chapter. Person first language is the dominant terminology in the global disability rights field (Shakespeare, 2013, p. 20). The term 'persons with disabilities' was broadly accepted by the international disability movement involved in drafting and negotiating the CRPD (Gooding, 2013). It is, however, worth noting that, although the CRPD adopts a social model approach to human rights, it does not reflect the language of the UK disabled peoples' movement (Oliver, 1990; Morris, 1991; Barnes, 1996; Thomas, 1999; Finkelstein, 2001; Shakespeare, 2013; Swain *et al.*, 2013).

There is no consensus on language preference within the broader disability movement in the UK. Some groups of activists, for example People First, have opted for the term 'people with learning difficulties'[8] emphasising that people are able to learn once disabling difficulties are overcome (Harris, 1995). The disabled people's movement in the UK uses the term 'disability' not to mean impairment but to refer to the disabling barriers of prejudice, discrimination and social exclusion: 'disabled people are those with impairments who are disabled by society' (Morris, 2001, p. 2).

While recognising the importance of language, it is arguably not as important as underlying values and can act as a diversion from the primary cause of promoting inclusion and rights of disabled people (Shakespeare, 2013). In keeping with the social model of disability, the term 'disabled people' will be used in this chapter in its widest sense to include people with physical, sensory, intellectual, cognitive and psychosocial impairments.

Independent living

The struggle for independent living was hard fought by disabled people and their allies (Barnes and Mercer, 2006). The concept of independent living underpins much of Scotland's recent social care legislation as it relates to disabled people.[9]

---

8   Available from URL: http://ncdj.org/2016/01/journalists-should-learn-to-carefully-traverse-a-variety-of-disability-terminology (accessed 16 February 2018).

9   For example, the statutory guidance to accompany the Social Care (Self-Directed Support) (Scotland) Act 2013 states: 'Independent living means people of all ages having the same freedom, choice, dignity and control as other citizens at home, at work, and in the community. It does not mean living by yourself, or fending for yourself. It means having rights to practical assistance and support to participate in society and live an ordinary life ... Self-directed support, alongside other policies, is intended to support, promote and protect human rights and independent living of care and support users in Scotland. It aims

The struggle to achieve this level of recognition grew from direct action in the early 1960s and 1970s by disabled activists who challenged the systematic exclusion and segregation on which most disability services were based. Their aim was to 'extend the range of control over our lives' (Hunt, 1981), ultimately leading to the realisation that 'community based alternatives to residential homes [are] an essential component of regaining the citizenship rights of disabled people' (Finkelstein, 1991, p. 35). Disabled activists argued:

> In our view, it is society which disables physically impaired people. Disability is something imposed on top of our impairments, by the way we are unnecessarily isolated and excluded from full participation by society (UPIAS, 1975).

Campaigners have continued to challenge systemic prejudice against disabled people by seeking to 'denaturalise forms of social oppression, demonstrating that what was thought of as natural was a product of specific social relations and ways of thinking' (Shakespeare, 2013, p. 12).

Further successes came with the formation of the Independent Living Fund in the 1980s, which provided disabled people with greater control over the resources required to organise any additional support required.[10] This was followed by the Community Care (Direct Payments) Act 1996, subsequently superseded in Scotland by the Social Care (Self-Directed Support) (Scotland) Act 2013. The Disability Discrimination Acts of 1995 and 2005 aimed to ensure public buildings and transport became more accessible. The Equality Act 2010 streamlined, strengthened and harmonised anti-discriminatory legislation seeking to provide the UK with a new discrimination law, which protects individuals from unfair treatment and promotes a fair and more equal society.[11] The concept of independent living has proved a consistent unifying basis upon which the disability movement has sought to achieve equality. It connects civil and political rights, control over one's life and equal participation in the community with economic and social rights, the need for requisite financial and prac-

to ensure that care and support is delivered in a way that supports choice and control over one's own life and which respects the person's right to participate in society'. Available from URL: www.gov.scot/Publications/2014/04/5438 (accessed 16 February 2018).

10 Available through ILF Scotland for Scotland and Northern Ireland but now closed in England and Wales. Available from URL: http://ilf.scot (accessed 16 February 2018).

11 Available from URL: www.gov.uk/guidance/equality-act-2010-guidance (accessed 16 February 2018).

tical support to make these rights a reality (Crowther, 2017). However, independence, autonomy and capacity are contested concepts, and it is to an exploration of this we now turn.

Liberty and autonomy

Autonomy can be understood as free will in the most basic sense (Coggon and Miola, 2011). Liberty, in contrast, represents the freedom to act without interference of a third party. A prisoner may have autonomy to express his will but little liberty to effect these choices and preferences. A person with significant mental disability may have low-level autonomy with limited ability to express his or her will; however, what will s/he can express can be given effect, realising a potentially high level of liberty. The traditional medico-juridical conception of autonomy and decision-making emphasises these individualistic aspects, informed by ideas of the rational, isolated and independent (Coggon and Miola, 2011). The most commonly used definition of competent decision-making regards the individual as an ideal, unencumbered and independent decision-maker (Beauchamp and Childress, 1994). In response, it has been suggested that a relational approach recognising that people rely on others for support and assistance in reaching decisions may provide a more faithful reflection of our common experience (Mackenzie and Stoljar, 2000). A relational autonomy approach lends credence to a supported decision-making model. Autonomy, or its legal counterpart legal capacity, is not assessed as a quality in the individual in isolation, rather in the context of appropriate support and assistance. In this iteration, mental capacity does not reside in the individual alone but in the response of society. The tension between the medico-juridical and relational approaches to capacity are mirrored in the differences between the medical and social theoretical models of disability to which we now turn.

Medical model and social model of disability

Historically, the medical model dominated the theoretical understanding of the concept of disability. Drawing on the disease model of medicine, disability is a consequence of a physiological or disease process (Oliver, 1990; Finkelstein, 1991; Shakespeare, 2013). Viewed as an aberration from the norm of human physiology and function, disability is regarded as an abnormality to be treated and mitigated against (Morris, 1991).

The disabled person by extension is regarded as flexible and alterable, while society is fixed and unalterable; the requirement to adapt or fit in therefore resides with the disabled person (Llewellyn and Hogan, 2000).

The social model of disability emerged to challenge the dominant medical model. It highlights the distinction between impairment (being the functional limitation within the individual) and disability (being the loss of opportunity due to physical and social barriers). The social model provides that it is society's failure to accommodate the needs of people with impairments which gives rise to the 'disabling disadvantage that people ... encounter in their daily lives, not some inherent mental, sensory or physical condition' (Bach and Kerzner, 2010, p. 14). Challenging the assumption of a value-free social world and the resultant pathologising of disability, the social model argues that disability is socially produced and that 'disability lies in the construction of society, not in the physical condition of the individual' (Drake, 1999). In keeping with the feminist movement's position that 'anatomy is not destiny', the disability movement asserts that the quality of disabled people's lives should not be determined by what their bodies cannot do, what they look like or how their minds function (Morris, 2013). The social model of disability informed the previously detailed developments in disability-related law, policy and practice by providing tools to challenge discrimination and prejudice, and a lexicon to describe the personal experience of impairment Morris (2001). The scope of influence of the social model of disability will become more apparent when considering the historical development of the ECHR and the CRPD.

Historical development – human rights and disability

The Second World War was a catalyst for the creation of the UN Charter, Article 55 of which required States to promote 'universal respect for, and observance of, human rights and fundamental freedoms for all without distinction as to race, sex, language or religion.'[12] The UDHR provided a 'catalogue of human rights and fundamental freedoms' (Rainey *et al.*, 2014, p. 3).

The ECHR draws heavily upon the rights outlined in the UDHR but goes beyond merely duplicating them. The development of the ECHR

---

12 Available from URL: www.cirp.org/library/ethics/UN-charter (accessed 16 February 2018).

was influenced by two key societal drivers: the desire to prevent the worst atrocities of the Second World War from recurring; and the perceived need to provide a bulwark against the spread of communism. It was recognised that additional rights would be added over time to ensure that the Convention was not static but instead would embody the idea of a 'living instrument'.

During the Second World War, disabled people, along with other identified social groups such as Jews, Roma people and homosexuals, were singled out for persecution and eradication under the Nazi regime, which regarded them as lesser citizens. The UN Charter was drawn up, in part, as a response to these atrocities. It makes clear the universal nature of human rights, although it has to be recognised that the long shadow of eugenics informed much policy and practice in relation to disabled people in the postwar period. It is imperative that one takes account of the culture that informed the drafting and development of the ECHR when reviewing its efficacy in defending the human rights of disabled people.

European Convention on Human Rights (ECHR)

As previously detailed in Chapter 1, the ECHR is primarily, although not exclusively, an instrument of civil and political rights. The strength of the ECHR in relation to disability has been the protection of individuals with a mental disorder, under Articles 3, 5 and 8, from unnecessary or uninvited treatment and detention and ensuring fair procedures when matters are adjudicated. Article 5(e), the right to liberty and security, provides for 'the lawful detention of persons for the prevention of the spreading of diseases, of persons of unsound mind, alcoholics or drug addicts or vagrants', which appears on the face of it to endorse detention based on cognitive impairment. The right to legal capacity is not expressly mentioned in the ECHR; the closest equivalent is found in Article 8(1), which has been interpreted to include the right to respect for physical and moral integrity and autonomy, *Bensaid v. United Kingdom*.[13] Article 8 of the ECHR enables legal capacity to be removed, provided it is lawful, proportionate and in pursuit of a legitimate aim such as the protection of health or to protect others. This approach forms the basis for Scottish mental health

---

13 *Bensaid v. United Kingdom* (44599/98) (2001) 33 EHRR 10.

and incapacity legislation,[14] which is currently undergoing a process of review and more about which is discussed later in this chapter.

The ECtHR has, historically, been relatively silent on issues relating to disability and capacity. Early notable case decisions included establishing the fact that detention, even if perceived to be voluntary, may still be unlawful, *De Wilde, Ooms and Versyp v. The Government of Belgium*.[15] The court also identified three criteria for the lawful detention of persons of unsound mind: (1) even if a person of unsound mind consented to such a deprivation of liberty, this would have to be subject to judicial decision; (2) the mental disorder(s) in question must be recognised by impartial medical expertise; and (3) the mental disorders must be extreme, *Winterwerp v. Netherlands*.[16]

Despite these cases, jurisprudence on legal capacity was significantly underdeveloped, although over the last five years or so this has begun to change (Series, 2015). An inherent tension exists between how best to respect the rights of people with impaired decision-making capacity and the question of how to do so proportionately. The ECtHR has found that a deprivation of legal capacity may amount to interference with the right to private life (Article 8(1)), *X and Y v. Croatia*,[17] even where it is partial, *Salontaji-Drobnjak v. Serbia*.[18] It has also found that the indiscriminate and comprehensive denial of legal capacity and the imposition of guardianship for persons with mental health issues violates Article 8, *Shtukaturov v. Russia*.[19] The question of legal identity is crucial in this regard:

> the tension is whether treating people with impaired decision making capacity as rights-bearing citizens is best done by minimising the extent to which there is formal legal intervention in their life, or whether de facto intervention which happens routinely in the lives of people should always require judicial authorisation (McKay, 2015).

14 Adults with Incapacity (Scotland) Act 2000; Mental Health Care and Treatment Act 2003; Adult Support and Protection (Scotland) Act 2007.

15 *De Wilde, Ooms and Versyp v. The Government of Belgium* (1971) 1 EHRR 373.

16 *Winterwerp v. Netherlands* (6301/73) [1979] ECHR 4.

17 *X and Y v. Croatia* (5193/09) [2011] ECHR 1835.

18 *Salontaji-Drobnjak v. Serbia* (36500/05) [2009] ECHR 1526.

19 *Shtukaturov v. Russia* (App. No. 44009/05) [2008] ECHR 223.

The CRPD appears to take the former position and is increasingly being used to reinforce ECHR rights in cases involving persons with mental disorders by the ECtHR (Slavert, 2013, p. 211). This tension runs through much of the debate in this area of human rights law: 'fundamentally there are two choices before humankind. One recognises that all persons have legal capacity and the other contends that legal capacity is not a universal human attribute' (Dhanda, 2006, p. 457). The CRPD is proving influential in informing the direction of travel in this regard, as will be illustrated in the following sections.

UN Convention on the Rights of Persons with Disabilities (CRPD)

The CRPD and its Optional Protocol[20] came into force on 3 May 2008, and the UK government ratified them on 8 June 2009 and 7 August, respectively.[21] The unanimous signing by all member States of the United Nations heralded a globally agreed consensus on a new approach to disability. As the first human rights treaty to be adopted in the twenty-first century, the CRPD signalled a 'paradigm shift' described by the then UN Secretary General Kofi Annan as 'the dawn of a new era – an era in which disabled people will no longer have to endure the discriminatory practices and attitudes that have been permitted to prevail for too long'.[22]

The CRPD is monitored at an international level through its treaty body, the UN Committee on the Rights of Persons with Disabilities (CRPD Committee). It is noteworthy that the CRPD is the first international human rights treaty to explicitly list a set of guiding principles; these are set out in Article 3.[23] It is also significant that, unlike most international human rights treaties, economic, social and cultural rights appear alongside civil and political rights.

The CRPD is also the first treaty to oblige State parties to take measures to eliminate discrimination 'by any person, organization or private

---

20 United Nations, Convention on the Rights of Persons with Disabilities and Optional Protocol, opened for signature 13 September 2006, GA Res 61/106; UN Doc A/Res/61/106 (entered into force 3 May 2008).

21 www.gov.uk/government/publications/un-convention-on-the-rights-of-persons-with-disabilities-initial-report-on-how-the-uk-is-implementing-it (accessed 12 March 2018).

22 UN Press Release: 'Secretary general hails adoption of landmark convention on the rights of people with disabilities', 13 December 2006. Available from URL: www.un.org/News/Press/docs/2006/sgsm10797.doc.htm (accessed 16 February 2018).

23 *supra* n. 19, p. 102.

enterprise',[24] by implication taking human rights law into the private sphere for the first time. It also, in Article 4(1), requires State parties to 'take into account the protection and promotion of the human rights of persons with disabilities in all policies and programmes', placing a wide-ranging obligation on State parties to ensure rights are protected, respected and fulfilled across the public and private spheres. The Convention's overall purpose is outlined as: 'to promote, protect and ensure the full and equal enjoyment of all human rights and fundamental freedoms by all persons with disabilities, and to promote respect for their inherent dignity'.[25] The Convention does not provide a definition of disability, but it details the wide scope that may be considered:

> Persons with disabilities include those who have long-term physical, mental, intellectual or sensory impairments which in interaction with the various barriers may hinder their full and effective participation in society on an equal basis with other.[26]

The right to independent living as part of the community is guaranteed in Article 19 of the UN Disability Convention. Article 19 provides that disabled people have the right to choose how they live their lives, to be fully included and to participate in society. It focuses particularly on the right to decide where you live and with whom. The focus is on the right to live in a community in a manner that supports and fosters inclusion and participation. The requirement for appropriate support to be available is highlighted, as well as the need for everyday supports to be accessible for disabled people. The Council of Europe Commissioner for Human Rights, in his recommendation on the right to independent living stated:

> The overarching objective of Article 19 of the CRPD is full inclusion and participation in society. Its three key elements are: choice; individualised supports that promote inclusion and prevent isolation: and making services for the general public accessible to people with disabilities (Commissioner for Human Rights, 2012).

Among other things, Article 19 has been said to establish a strong pre-

---

24 *supra* n. 19, Article 4(1)(e).
25 CRPD Article 1(1).
26 CRPD but Article 1(2).

sumption against long-term institutional care, so is in favour of de-institutionalisation. As the Council of Europe Commissioner stated:

> This right is violated when people with disabilities who need some form of support in their everyday lives are required to relinquish living in the community in order to receive that support; when support is provided in a way that takes away people's control from their own lives; when support is altogether withheld, thus confining a person to the margins of the family or society; or when the burden is placed on people with disabilities to fit into public services and structures rather than these services and structures being designed to accommodate the diversity of the human condition (Commissioner for Human Rights, 2012, p. 5).

To an extent, the ECHR and the CRPD reflect the cultural roots they were drawn from: the ECHR emphasises judicial oversight while the CRPD emphasises autonomy and discourages any attempt to use legal processes to substitute for decision-making of the individual. Recent interpretations by the Committee on the Rights of Persons with Disabilities (the Committee) have only reinforced these differences. For example, General Comment No. 1 (2014) interpreting Article 12 brought the issue of possession of legal capacity and its exercise into sharper relief for persons with mental health issues when stating:

> The concept of mental capacity is highly controversial in and of itself. Mental capacity is not, as is commonly presented, an objective, scientific and naturally occurring phenomenon. Mental capacity is contingent on social and political contexts, as are the disciplines, professions and practices which play a dominant role in assessing mental capacity.[27]

The differences in approach adopted by the ECHR and the CRPD serve to reinforce the idea that the law should not be regarded as value neutral – the law reinforces certain relationship structures and power dynamics.

27 Committee on the Rights of Persons with Disabilities (2014) 'General comment No. 1 (2014): Article 12: Equal recognition before the law' (online). Available from URL: http://tbinternet.ohchr.org/_layouts/treatybodyexternal/Download.aspx?symbolno=CRPD/C/GC/1&Lang=en (accessed 12 March 2018). Geneva: Committee on the Rights of Persons with Disabilities.

The cultural context of the ECHR, written in the shadow of the Second World War and informed by thinking influenced by eugenics, contrasts sharply with the aspirations of the CRPD. The latter, informed as it was by the views of disabled people and rooted in the ideals of independent living, challenges existing disabling legal, structural and cultural norms. It embodies the aspiration to achieve true equality for disabled people.

Separate mental health legislation is common across legal jurisdictions. Such legislation typically authorises compulsory/involuntary hospitalisation and treatment in the case of those with mental disorder of a sufficient level of seriousness. It is argued that this approach treats people with mental disability, as defined by law, according to a different set of legal principles as applied to those not so defined – an approach that could be regarded as discriminatory (Richardson, 2012). The CRPD rejection of a 'best interests' approach – one enshrined in the UNCRC[28] – has implications for jurisdictions worldwide that have adopted this principle in national legislation to underpin substitute decision-making regimes in relation to those deemed to lack 'functional' capacity. Article 12 of the Convention recognises that persons with disabilities have legal capacity on an equal basis with others. Simply put, an individual cannot lose his/her legal capacity to act simply because of a disability. Legal capacity can be lost in situations that apply to everyone, such as if someone is convicted of a crime.[29]

The UN Convention, while binding on the UK in international law, does not have the same status domestically as the ECHR. There has been no process of incorporation and the enforcement mechanisms available to ensure compliance are diplomatic rather than legal. The UK signed up to the Optional Protocol, which allows access to the Committee on the Rights of Persons with Disabilities, to individuals and groups who claim to be the victims of violation of the provisions of the Convention. All means of redress in the UK and the ECtHR must have been exhausted first and, in the face of an adverse finding,

---

28 Convention on the Rights of the Child, adopted by UN GA Res 44/25 on 20 November 1989, Article 3(1).

29 Available from URL: www.un.org/development/desa/disabilities/resources/handbook-for-parliamentarians-on-the-convention-on-the-rights-of-persons-with-disabilities/chapter-six-from-provisions-to-practice-implementing-the-convention.html (accessed 16 February 2018).

international reputational damage would be the primary sanction. This has led some commentators to suggest that the primary value of the Convention should be regarded as expressive, educational and proactive (Lewis, 2010).

The impact of human rights law on mental health law is best illustrated by the ongoing influence of the CRPD on the developing understanding of the concept of capacity. The CRPD's approach to legal capacity profoundly challenges the medico-juridical formulation of the rights and duties afforded to persons with disabilities. This approach is most clearly articulated through the idea of mental capacity as a threshold of perceived decision-making competence, which determines access to autonomous decision-making. Alternative, substitute, decision-making arrangements are made should the threshold not be met. In this respect, it has been argued that 'the concept of mental capacity has the dual function of protecting an individual's right of autonomy and safeguarding their welfare should they be found to lack capacity' (Kong, 2015).

Jurisdictions worldwide use 'mental capacity' as a determining characteristic for granting or denying legal capacity. Assessments of 'mental capacity' frequently include an assessment about an individual's impairment or disability. As Article 12(2) requires that the enjoyment of legal capacity be equal, any assessment based upon impairment or disability would, on the face of it, be discriminatory. Article 12(3) of the CRPD introduces an obligation on State parties 'to take appropriate measures to provide access by persons with disabilities to the support they may require in exercising their legal capacity'. Article 12(4) outlines the safeguards required for all measures that relate to legal capacity, stating in part that:

> Such safeguards shall ensure that the measures relating to the exercise of legal capacity respect the rights, will and preferences of the person, are free from conflict of interest and undue influence, are proportional and tailored to the person's circumstances, apply for the shortest time possible and are subject to regular review by a competent, independent and impartial authority or judicial body.[30]

Article 12, when read in full, clearly intimates that legal capacity should be uncoupled from mental capacity as a binary concept, with a move

---

30 *supra* n. 1, Article 12(4).

towards the increased use of supported decision-making. This upholds the position 'that one never really loses legal authority to make decisions; instead, support for decision-making becomes ever stronger, as functional ability decreases' (Bartlett, 2014, p. 7).

The unequivocal stance taken by the CRPD and affirmed by General Comment No. 1 (2014)[31] poses significant challenges in the implementation. Fennell and Khaliq (2011) point out the conflict of laws that arise between the CRPD and Article 5 of the ECHR – the former requiring that disability form no part of the justification for a person's detention, and 'unsoundness of mind' forming someone permitted justification for deprivation of liberty under Article 5(1) of the latter. It should be noted that several State parties, including Australia and Canada, have entered reservations on the basis that Article 12 should be interpreted as allowing substitute decision-making in certain circumstances.[32]

The gap between the CRPD's values and the current reality of many mental health laws worldwide reflects, it has been suggested, a position 'where the CRPD is trying to set out a future reality which has as yet to be explained' (Lewis, 2010, p. 104).

UK national picture

Mental capacity/adult incapacity legislation is decentralised in the UK, with significant different legal provisions in each of the separate legal systems in Scotland, Northern Ireland, and England and Wales (the last forming one jurisdiction). The UK is currently experiencing an unprecedented law reform movement in relation to mental capacity/adult incapacity legislation (Martin, 2016, p. 5).

The Scottish picture

In Scotland, all devolved legislation (including secondary legislation) must be compatible with the ECHR.[33] All public authorities must act in a way that is compatible with ECHR obligations,[34] and courts and

---

31 Committee on the Rights of Persons with Disabilities (2014), *General Comment No. 1*, Geneva: UN.

32 Text of all reservations to the treaty are available from URL: https://treaties.un.org/ Pages/ViewDetails.aspx?src=TREATY&mtdsg_no=IV-15&chapter=4&clang=_en (accessed 16 February 2018).

33 Human Rights Act 1998, s.6; Scotland Act 1998, s.29(2)(d) and s.57.

34 Human Rights Act 1998, s.6(3)(b).

tribunals[35] need to have regard to the jurisprudence of the ECtHR.[36] On a technical legal basis, the Law Society of Scotland has noted that the proposals in the General Comment report could not be completely enacted in Scotland, where legislation incompatible with the ECHR would be ultra vires of the legislature.[37]

Scotland has a well-regarded mental health and incapacity regime based upon the Adults with Incapacity (Scotland) Act 2000 (AWI)[38] and the Mental Health (Care and Treatment) (Scotland) Act 2003 (MHA)[39] and the Adult Support and Protection (Scotland) Act 2007 (ASP).[40] The purpose of adult incapacity legislation is to promote and safeguard the rights and interests of adults whose ability to do so for themselves is impaired by incapacity. The AWI and the MHA predate the UK's ratification of the CRPD. Consequently, both the evolving nature of ECtHR jurisprudence and the implications of CRPD Article 12 pose significant challenges for compliance with human rights obligations.

Adults with Incapacity (Scotland) Act 2000 (AWI)

The AWI introduced a system for safeguarding the welfare and managing the finances and property of adults who lack capacity to act or to make decisions for themselves, because of mental illness, learning disability, dementia or other condition (or inability to communicate due to physical condition).[41] It is based upon five key principles: that the intervention will benefit the adult; be the least restrictive option; the intervention should take account of the present and past wishes and feelings of the adult so far as can be ascertained; consultation should take place with relevant others; and that the intervention should encourage the person to use existing skills and develop new skills.[42]

---

35 Human Rights Act 1998, s.6(3)(a).

36 Human Rights Act 1998, s.2.

37 Law Society of Scotland response to Committee on the Rights of Persons with Disabilities (UN) draft General Comment on Article 12 of the Convention – Equal Recognition before the Law and Draft General Comment on Article 9 of the Convention, 2013.

38 Scottish Executive (2000b) *Adults with Incapacity (Scotland) Act 2000*, Edinburgh: The Stationery Office.

39 Scottish Parliament (2003) 'Mental Health (Care and Treatment) (Scotland) Act 2003'.

40 Scottish Executive (2007) *Adult Support and Protection (Scotland) Act 2007*, Edinburgh: Scottish Executive.

41 Mental Welfare Commission for Scotland (2015) 'AWI Act monitoring 2014/15'. Available from URL: www.mwcscot.org.uk/media/240694/awi_monitoring_report__2__2014-15.pdf (accessed 12 March 2018).

42 Available from URL: www.legislation.gov.uk/asp/2000/4/contents (accessed 16 February

It introduced a new and comprehensive process of substitute decision-making in the form of court-appointed guardians or attorneys appointed for the person to act on their behalf. The explicit aim of the legislation was to maximise the autonomy of the individual. There was no expectation that guardianship should be applied to all those who lacked capacity, and informal arrangements could be made to provide ongoing care and support. Difficulties associated with the lack of legal recognition for these arrangements, however, have become increasingly obvious.[43] The Mental Welfare Commission for Scotland (MWC) has safeguarding duties in relation to people who fall under the protection of the AWI.

Routine monitoring by the MWC for the period 2014/15 has highlighted worrying trends in the practical implementation of the AWI.[44] The number of new guardianship applications continues to increase, with a 16% rise in new applications granted. Private ones accounted for 76% of all applications, local authorities the other 24%. The Scotland rate for approved welfare guardianships rose from 48 per 100,000 to 55 per 100,000 in the over sixteen age group. Of significance is that, for the first time, the number of applications for adults with learning disabilities was greater (45%) than that for people with dementia. Even more concerning, 21% of the welfare guardianships granted in 2014/15 were for learning disabled young adults aged 16–24 years. The lack of automatic periodical judicial scrutiny of approved orders places the onus on the individual or another interested party to challenge the order; the MWC notes this rarely happens.[45] There is significant potential for a breach of ECHR Article 5, where indefinite guardianship is used to authorise deprivation of liberty, as European case law makes clear the need for regular review.[46]

One of the unintended consequences of the Social Care (Self-Directed Support) (Scotland) Act 2013 has been a spike in private applications for welfare guardianship by parents of learning disabled adults. Where an individual cannot consent to their proposed package of support, someone else with formal proxy powers is required, with the local authorities' approval, to make the arrangements. Currently, formal guardianship applications may be required for informal carers such

2018).
43 supra n. 19, p. 4.
44 supra n. 19.
45 supra n. 19, p. 15.
46 Stanev v. Bulgaria (2012) 55 EHRR 696 paras 124–128.

as parents and family members to continue in this role.[47] The MWC has highlighted concerns that 'requiring court authorisation for such arrangements is a potentially complex and cumbersome mechanism ... [and] should be considered in ongoing consideration of the 2000 Act'.[48]

In terms of CRPD Article 12 compliance, Scottish capacity law still permits decisions which could conflict with the person's own will and preferences based on a functional assessment of mental capacity and as such would not comply with the General Comment interpretation of Article 12. Research has identified the influence of the assessor on the outcome of the assessment, introducing a questionable level of arbitrariness (Raymont *et al.*, 2007). There is a marked tendency to conflate the determination of capacity with the outcome of the decision, known as the 'concertina effect' whereby people who agree with care-providing authorities are more likely to be assumed to have capacity (Williams *et al.*, 2012). These influences reinforce concerns about using a 'bright line' binary notion of capacity as a threshold for the determination of human rights safeguards.

The AWI was crafted to give primacy to the 'will and preferences' of the adult and their best interpretation; however, legal commentators note a disappointing trend 'away from a "constructed decisions" approach, towards a "best interests" approach in the sense used, and criticised, by the UN Committee' (Keene and Ward, 2016, p. 36). This offers a clear example of the limitations of the law in changing behaviour in practice in a way that directly impacts disabled people in receipt of health or social care.

AWI was built on human rights foundations, drawing on the global trend towards a more individualised, functional and person-centred approach to assessing whether an individual has capacity to make decisions. This means that the existence of a learning disability, even a quite profound one, would not of itself be determinative of capacity to make a decision. It applies the proportionality test in the interference with the right to a private and family life and requires that any intervention in the affairs of an adult is the 'least restrictive option in relation to the freedom of the adult, consistent with the purposes of the intervention'.[49] This accords with the ECHR jurisprudence requiring a

---

47 Available from URL: www.legislation.gov.uk/asp/2013/1/notes/division/3/4/4
   (accessed 12 March 2018).
48 *supra* n. 19.
49 Adults with Incapacity (Scotland) Act 2000, s.1(3).

'tailor made approach'.[50] Despite these solid foundations, regarded as world leading at the time, the requirement built into the HRA that all legislation be viewed through the ECHR has meant that this legislation has not kept up to date with developments (SHRC, 2016a). The Office of the Public Guardian expressed serious concerns about the viability of the current guardianship regime, noting that the 'use of interim guardians, use of indefinite orders and the granting of unnecessary welfare powers arguably breach human rights legislation' and has suggested the adoption of a more explicitly HRBA.[51] The Scottish Government's *Mental Health Strategy: 2017–2027* explicitly states (in Point 34) its intention to 'Reform Adults With Incapacity (AWI) legislation' (Scottish Government, 2017a, p. 6).

Mental Health Care and Treatment (Scotland) Act 2003 (MHA)

The purpose of the MHA is to provide an updated legislative framework for compulsory treatment of people with mental disorder, a term which includes people who have a mental illness, learning disability or related condition. Section 259 incorporates the right to access independent advocacy services for any person with a mental disorder, regardless of whether they are subject to compulsory measures.[52] This safeguard is, however, contingent upon the availability of the service and concerns have been raised regarding the inadequacies of such provision across Scotland.[53]

The SHRC, in its response to the draft mental health strategy 2016, suggested that:

> the Code of Practice accompanying the Mental Health (Care and Treatment) (Scotland) Act 2003 should be revised to involve explicit connections to human rights principles and to the human rights framework. Doing so will help to embed rights based practice (SHRC, 2016a, p. 9).

---

50 *Shtukaturov v. Russia* (App. No. 44009/05) [2008] ECHR.

51 Office of the Public Guardian (2011) 'Early deliberations of graded guardianship', November 2011.

52 *supra* n. 37, p. 307.

53 Scottish Independent Advocacy Alliance (2014) *Response to Call for Evidence on Mental Health (Scotland) Bill to Scottish Parliament Health and Sports Committee*, MHB030, Edinburgh: Scottish Independent Advocacy Alliance.

The Scottish Government's *Mental Health Strategy: 2017–2027* explicitly states (at Point 32) the intention to 'use a rights-based approach in the statutory guidance on the use of mental health legislation' (Scottish Government, 2017a, p. 6).

Section 13ZA of the Social Work (Scotland) Act 1968

A 2007 amendment to the Social Work (Scotland) Act 1968 empowers local authorities to take any necessary steps to help an adult benefit from a service without further judicial review. This should only occur in circumstances where an assessment of need has taken place and where consensus exists that an individual requires a community-care service but is not capable of making the decision. Disability advocacy groups have raised concerns about the potential misuse of these wide-ranging powers – specifically, the lack of monitoring and oversight, which may breach ECHR Article 5 (which prohibits detention without a proper process of law) if the circumstance amount to a deprivation of liberty.[54]

Case Example: HL v. UK (2005)

The Bournewood case, adjudicated on by the ECtHR as *HL v. UK* (2005)[55] is of relevance. The case concerned an individual who had been treated on a reputed informal basis in a psychiatric hospital but against the wishes of his carers, who had been deprived of access to him. The ECtHR determined that the admission to the psychiatric hospital and continued residence there of a person with learning disabilities, such that he could not consent to being where he was, represented a deprivation of liberty, could not be characterised as voluntary and needed to take place under a lawful process to comply with Article 5. A key factor in determining deprivation of liberty was that those treating and managing the person exercise complete control over that person's care and movements and that they are not free to leave.[56] A similar conclusion was reached in a more recent case of *Stanev v. Bulgaria*. Whether a person is in a 'locked' or 'lockable' environment is relevant but not determinative.[57] This decision led to significant review of mental health and capacity legislation across the UK and to the introduction of Deprivation of Liberty Safeguards (DOLS) in the Mental Capacity Act 2005 in England and Wales, in an effort to bridge the 'Bournewood gap'.

---

54 Available from URL: www.siaa.org.uk/wp-content/uploads/2014/03/SIAA_
    Spring_2014.pdf (accessed 12 March 2018).
55 *HL v. UK* [2005] EHRR 32.
56 ibid., para 91.
57 *Stanev v. Bulgaria* (2012) 55 EHRR 696 paras 124–8.

Adopting a HRBA to the circumstances of this case by applying the PANEL principles raises several practice considerations. A focus on facilitating greater meaningful participation on the part of the individual and their family/informal carers might have avoided such an adversarial situation developing. Consensus is not always possible, however; recognising the value of family and independent advocate involvement can prevent situations escalating. All engaged parties being accountable for the decisions made and committing to communicating these in an honest, clear and transparent manner may allow disagreements to be dealt with early in deliberations. Consciously questioning whether proposed actions would apply to any citizen may also provide a helpful check as to whether the decisions are being made on a non-discriminatory basis. If, as a practitioner or family member, the outcome of a decision being considered would only apply to a disabled person, an HRBA would require that decision to be reconsidered. Unless there were active concerns that family members were engaging in an abusive relationship, alienating family members is not empowering. Even in circumstances where abuse is a genuine concern, the individual should, where possible, participate in establishing the terms of ongoing contact, and a legal framework should be in place to support any such restrictions.

Adult Support and Protection (Scotland) Act 2007 (ASP)
The ASP seeks to protect and benefit adults at risk of being harmed. The Act requires councils and a range of public bodies to work together to support and protect adults who are unable to safeguard themselves, their property and their rights.[58] It introduced several measures to improve protection for adults at risk of harm – broadly defined to include physical, psychological, financial and self-harm (Patrick, 2009). The ASP defines adults at risk as those who:

- are unable to safeguard their own well-being, property, rights or other interests;
- are at risk of harm;
- are more vulnerable to being harmed than adults who are not so affected, because they are affected by disability, mental disorder, illness or physical or mental infirmity.

---

58 Available from URL: www.gov.scot/Topics/Health/Support-Social-Care/Adult-Support-Protection (accessed 16 February 2018).

AWI s.3(5a) was added to the ASP and it provides a principle which is subsidiary to AWI s.1(4)(a), for the purposes of ascertaining the adult's wishes and feelings for sheriff court proceedings, by requiring the sheriff to take account of them as expressed by an independent advocate. The AWI authorises the sheriff, in addition to appointing a safeguarder, to appoint a person to ascertain and convey to the court the views of the adult (AWI s.3(5)). Concerns have been expressed that duplication exists between the AWI (in 2000) and the ASP (in 2007), leading to risks that individuals fall between two agencies both having considered that the other is undertaking their duty to investigate.

Although founded on human rights principles such as participation, empowerment and non-discrimination, concerns have been raised that the ASP embodies a paternalistic legacy. The Campaign for a Fair Society – a coalition of disabled people's organisations and organisations that support disabled people – highlighted that the ASP gives local authorities the power to remove an adult at risk from their home and place them somewhere else where they can be protected, thereby removing the adult at risk from their home rather than the person suspected of placing them at risk. It is argued that this potentially violates their right to privacy and to private home and family life (Campaign for a Fair Society, 2012).

The CRPD sets forth an ambitious and laudable challenge to nation states that have ratified the Convention. The progressive realisation of the rights enshrined will require State parties to review legislation, policy and practice. Some 172 countries have ratified the CRPD, but none can claim to be CRPD compliant. Scotland's mental health legislation requires to be reviewed. The ECHR is a 'living instrument', the interpretation of which depends upon the prevailing standards of the time and 'Strasbourg jurisprudence is moving well beyond Article 5 in its engagement with the rights of people perceived as lacking capacity' (Bartlett, 2014, p. 3).

The question for Scotland in terms of law and practice in the fields of health and social care and disability is whether it wants to lead by example or follow and change only when required to be compliant? The CRPD has been informing developments in mental health and capacity regimes across the globe. There are opportunities to develop Scotland's law, policy and practice by learning from other jurisdictions.

Practice Example: Canada: Supported Decision-Making

Canadian adult guardi both substitute and supported decision-making in Canada's legal framework anship law reform has included measures to provide supported decision-making and other forms of support to exercise legal capacity. The Canadian government, through its declaration and reservation[59] in relation to the CRPD, made clear its intention to maintain (Kerzner, 2011). Bach and Kerzner, Article 12 scholars, proposed to the Ontario Law Commission that legislation to support the exercise of legal capacity and comply with Article 12 should recognise three approaches to exercising legal capacity (Bach and Kerzner, 2010). The first is defined as 'legally independent status', whereby the individual requires only minor accommodations such as accessible information (ibid., p. 83). The second is categorised as 'supported-decision making status', where individual support persons are appointed to assist an individual in making decisions and/or representing the person to ensure their will and preferences are known (ibid., p. 87). The third is 'facilitated-decision making status', which requires others to facilitate the making of needed decisions (ibid., p. 91). In this case, a facilitator will interpret the will and preferences of the individual and make good faith representation (ibid., pp. 91–4). This approach offers a more nuanced or graded consideration of decision-making based upon an explicitly relational approach.

Practice and Legal Example: England: Deprivation of Liberty (DoLS)

In England and Wales, as a response to the outcome of *HL v. United Kingdom*, the government passed the so-called 'deprivation of liberty' (DOLS) safeguards[60] to regulate the deprivation of liberty of adults lacking capacity in hospitals, care homes and other settings. The *Cheshire West v. Chester Council* case interpreted the scope of deprivation of liberty in a far broader sense than previous jurisprudence, resulting in a vast increase in DOLS applications. This judgement considered whether a deprivation of liberty occurred in the case of an 'incapable' adult even where there was appropriate and least restrictive care available.

Two cases were combined in the Cheshire West judgement. The first *Surrey County Council v. CA, LA, MIG and MEG*[61] involved two young women in the care of a local authority. The second case, *Cheshire West*

---

59 Available from URL: https://treaties.un.org/Pages/ViewDetails.
    aspx?src=TREATY&mtdsg_no=IV-15&chapter=4&clang=_en#EndDec (accessed 12 March 2018).
60 For more detail on DOLS see: Bartlett, P. and Sandland, R. (2014) *Mental Health Law: Policy and Practice* (4th edn), Oxford: Oxford University Press, chapter 5.
61 *Surrey Council v. CA, LA, Mig and Meg* [2010] EWHC 785 (Fam) COP.

and Chester Council v. P[62] involved a man who had cerebral palsy and Down's Syndrome and required twenty-four-hour support. In each case, the Court of Appeal determined that the care and support arrangements did not constitute a deprivation of liberty.

The decisions in both cases were appealed to the Supreme Court. Lady Hale, who gave the leading judgement, rejected the idea that the concept of deprivation of liberty was any different for the appellants based on their disabilities and the consequent need for care and support. Her comments in paragraph 45 were unequivocal:

> In my view, it is axiomatic that people with disabilities, both mental and physical, have the same human rights as the rest of the human race. It may be that those rights have sometimes to be limited or restricted because of their disabilities, but the starting place should be the same as that for everyone else. This flows inexorably from the universal character of human rights, founded on the inherent dignity of all human beings, and is confirmed in the United Nations Convention on the Rights of Person with Disabilities.[63]

Lady Hale proposed an 'acid test' for deprivation of liberty cases. The view taken was that, if the person concerned is 'under continuous supervision and control and [is] not free to leave', this was the key determining characteristic. Freedom to leave was explained as the 'ability to move away without permission'. At its simplest reading, the Cheshire West judgement appears to offer a ringing endorsement of the CRPD position in relation to the inalienable and equal human rights of disabled people. It does, however, throw into doubt the legal basis of the care and support arrangements for many thousands of people who have been 'placed' in care settings outwith any legal framework.

The Bournewood and Cheshire West judgements pose significant challenges to mental health legislative, policy and practice arrangements. In 2014, the Report of the MCA Post-Legislative Scrutiny Committee of the House of Lords recommended that they be replaced entirely with a new system, following full consultation and parliamentary scrutiny.[64]

---

62 *Cheshire West and Chester Council v. P* [2014] UKSC 19, [2014] MHLO 16.

63 *P v. Cheshire West and Chester Council and another; (2) P and Q v. Surrey County Council* [2014] UKSC 19.

64 House of Lords Select Committee on the Mental Capacity Act 2005 (2014) *Mental Capacity Act 2005: Post Legislative Scrutiny* (HL Paper 139), London: The Stationery Office, para 258. Available from URL: https://publications.parliament.uk/pa/ld201314/ldselect/ldmentalcap/139/139.pdf (accessed 16 February 2018).

MCA Section 4(6) requires those who have to determine a person's best interests to consider in 'so far is reasonably ascertainable the person's past and present wishes and feelings'. There has been a shift in interpretation, most notably the Supreme court decision in *Aintree University Hospital NHS Foundation Trust v. James*,[65] in which Lady Hale emphasised that the best interests' test was 'to consider matters from the patient's point of view'.[66] Supreme Court rulings such as these are not binding on Scotland but are, nevertheless, influential.

Practice Example: Australia: Supported decision-making

In Australia, the Office of the Public Advocate of South Australia trialled a non-statutory supported decision-making programme. Supported decision-making was described as 'formal arrangements that go beyond the informal assistance of family and friends but stop short of substitute decision-making through guardianship, administration and Enduring Powers of Attorney'.[67] The aim of the pilot was to 'test supported decision-making as an early intervention strategy for people not under guardianship' which may 'prevent problems occurring in the future', thereby avoiding the need for guardianship orders.[68] An independent evaluation detailing the project's outcomes reported that it had achieved both outcomes, diverting people away from both welfare guardianship and administrative orders.[69] There is scope for policymakers and practitioners to draw on these international innovations to ensure that domestic legal and policy developments capture the aspiration of the CRPD.

Learning disability

In the year 2000, the Scottish government published the first national learning disability strategy entitled *The Same As You?* (Scottish Executive, 2000). An evaluation in 2012 recognised considerable progress in the process of deinstitutionalisation. It also noted that there required to be 'a much greater emphasis on support that builds people's capacity

---

65 *Aintree University Hospitals NHS Foundation Trust v. James* [2013] UKSC 67.

66 ibid., n. 229, para 45.

67 Office of the Public Advocate (2009) 'Supported decision-making: Background and discussion paper' (online). Available from URL: www.publicadvocate.vic.gov.au/our-services/publications-forms/carers/supported-decision-making/58-supported-decision-making-background-and-discussion-paper (accessed 16 February 2018).

68 ibid.

69 Wallace, M. (2012) 'Evaluation of the Supported Decision Making Project' (online), Office of the Public Advocate. Available from URL: www.opa.sa.gov.au/resources/supported_decision_making (accessed 16 February 2018).

to lead independent, healthy lives' (Scottish Government, 2012). It was reported that a significant number (869) of people with a learning disability under the age of fifty-five were resident in care homes for older people (Learning Disability Alliance Scotland, 2010).

It has been suggested that ECHR Article 8 is likely to become increasingly important (Bartlett, 2014) in such situations, as the following case illustrates.

Case Example: London Borough of Hillingdon v. Steven Neary

London Borough of Hillingdon v. Steven Neary[70] was a high-profile case involving a young disabled man, Steven, who lived with his father, Mark. The local authority accepted Steven into respite care for a few days at the request of his father, who was unwell and needed time to recuperate.

The local authority kept him for a year, against his wishes and those of his father. The legality of this action was the subject of the court case. In judgement, Justice Jackson was at pains to acknowledge that 'everybody concerned has genuinely wanted to do the right thing ... the problems arose from misjudgment, not from lack of commitment'.[71] The court found that Hillingdon had breached Steven Neary's rights, under ECHR Article 8, by preventing him from living with his father. The court noted the failure to carry out a genuinely balanced 'best interest' assessment and that there was:

> no acknowledgement of the unique bond between S[sic] and his father, or of the priceless importance to a dependent person of the personal element in care by a parent rather than a stranger, however committed.[72]

Hillingdon was also found to have breached Steven's rights under ECHR Article 5(1) by unlawfully depriving him of his liberty. The court found that by failing to adhere to the requirements of the MHA – by (1) securing an independent mental health advocate, (2) ensuring an effective review and (3) ensuring timely issue of proceedings – Hillingdon had failed in its obligations to Steven, which amounted to a breach of Article 5(4).

Viewing this case through the lens of the PANEL principles may help to identify alternative courses of action that would have been available had a HRBA been adopted. The full participation of those who knew and cared about Steven – in this case, his father – would have potentially avoided the development of an adversarial situation. Where

---

70 *London Borough of Hillingdon v. Steven Neary* [2011] EWHC 1377 (COP).

71 ibid., para 16.

72 *supra* n. 68, para 155(1).

concerns about a conflict of interest may have arisen, early involvement of an independent advocate to ensure the primacy of Steven's will and preferences may similarly have avoided an escalation of tensions. It was noted that 'Hillingdon's approach was calculated to prevent proper scrutiny of the situation it had created.'[73] Transparency, honesty and accountability would have potentially contributed to a speedier resolution of the outstanding issues. Steven's distress, articulated through his behaviour, was used as justification for his continued detention. The circular logic adopted in this situation is inherently discriminatory, requiring of disabled people that they communicate in a way that may be unavailable to them. A non-discriminatory approach would have ensured that the widest range of communication strategies were considered when trying to ascertain the person's will and preferences. In this case it may have involved recognising and respecting the role of people who knew Steven best, his family and his support workers, those who were most able to help Steven express his will and preferences. Hillingdon gave precedence to professional judgement over the empowerment of Steven and his family.

The court was clear that the:

> evidential burden is on the local authority to demonstrate that its arrangements are better than those that can be achieved within the family ... the fact that an individual does not bring a matter to court does not relieve the local authority of the obligation to act, it redoubles it.[74]

Ultimately, when significant disagreements occur, statutory safeguards should be activated and the legality of the action tested:

> the ordinary powers of a local authority are limited to investigating, providing support services and where appropriate referring matters to court. If a local authority seeks to regulate, control, compel, restrain, confine or coerce it must, except in emergency, point to the specific statutory authority for what it is doing or else obtain the appropriate sanction in court.[75]

Had this happened in the Neary case, Steven would not have spent a

---

73 *supra* n. 68, para 155(2).
74 *supra* n. 68, para 19.
75 *supra* n. 68, para 22.

year away from his family home, and Hillingdon would not have found itself on the wrong side of a high-profile human rights judgement.

ECHR Article 8 requires that everyone has the right to respect for a private and family life. CRPD Article 23 further specifies, with respect to people with physical, mental or learning disabilities, which State parties should 'take effective and appropriate measures to eliminate discrimination against persons with disabilities in all matters relating to marriage, family and parenthood and relationships on an equal basis with others'. In practice, the UN CESCR recognised that the right to marry and found a family is 'frequently ignored or denied, especially in the case of persons with [learning] disabilities' (UN CESCR, 1994). A 2012 evaluation of the Scottish government's learning disability strategy *Same as You?* noted that: 'Having more friends and the chance to have romantic and/or sexual relationships were among the priorities which people with learning disabilities chose for their lives' (Scottish Government, 2012). The complexities of this are succinctly summarised by the MWC when stating:

> People with a mental illness, learning disability or other mental disorder have the same personal and sexual needs and rights as anyone else ... At the same time, people with a mental disorder can be at particular risk of abuse or exploitation. Balancing those rights and risks raises a host of legal and moral dilemmas to which there are no easy solutions. While the motivation may be to protect, professionals and carers need to consider carefully whether any interference with an individual's rights is ethical, lawful, necessary and in proportion to the risks (MWC, 2010).

This balance of rights and risks is highlighted in the case example of *CH v. A Metropolitan Council*.

Case Example: CH v. A Metropolitan Council[76]

This case was, in substance, a claim for damages pursuant to the Human Rights Act 1998. CH is a married man with Down's Syndrome who, with his wife WH, sought fertility advice from a health service. He was assessed by a consultant psychologist who raised concerns regarding his capacity to consent to sexual relations and suggested a sexual education course

---

76 *CH v. A Metropolitan Council* [2017] EWCOP 12.

to assist him to achieve the necessary capacity. The psychologist, in turn, notified the local authority advising of the findings and the requirement for the educational course. The local authority responded by writing to WH advising that she must abstain from sex with her husband as it would comprise a serious sexual offence under Sections 30–1 of the Sexual Offences Act 2003. Given her concerns about the implications of potential safeguarding procedures, WH complied, moving into a separate bedroom and reducing any signs of physical affection. The local authority failed to provide the required sexual education input until required by an order of court some fifteen months later. The local authority was found to be in breach of Section 6(1) of the HRA, which provides: 'It is unlawful for a public authority to act in a way that is incompatible with a convention right' – the Convention right in this case was ECHR Article 8(1) the right to respect for private and family life.

Again, reflectively applying the PANEL principles to this scenario can help to determine whether alternative courses of action could have been taken had a HRBA been adopted. The couple's full participation in the process of assessment and deliberation would have provided the opportunity to clarify any misunderstandings early in the process. Accountability for and recognition of the impact that the intervention was having on the marital life of CH and WH would have required a speedy response to action the psychologist's recommendation. A non-discriminatory approach, for example asking whether this course of action would be applied to a non-disabled person, would have highlighted the inherently discriminatory basis of the failure to act timeously. Supporting CH and WH to develop a greater understanding of issues relating to their sexual health and well-being in a positive and proactive manner would have been more empowering. The level of State intervention and the impact experienced by CH and WH may seem inconceivable. For people with learning disabilities it is all too common; concerns have been raised about the failure of residential group homes to respect the level of privacy necessary to conduct normal adult relationships (Hollomotz, 2009).

Human rights based and person-centred approaches share the same starting point (a focus on the individual) and the same essential goal (the empowerment of individuals to exercise greater choice and control over life decisions) (Chetty, 2012).

Practice Example: Dates-n-Mates[77]

Dates-n-Mates is a Scottish-based dating and friendship agency run by and for people with learning disabilities. It adopts a HRBA to its work, supporting adults with learning disabilities to develop wider relationship networks both on an intimate and a friendship basis. The project was highlighted in the 2013 Scottish national ten-year learning disability strategy, 'The keys to life', as an example of good practice.[78]

Again using the PANEL principles, the project encourages full participation, being run by and for people with learning disabilities. It is accountable to its members through a range of participatory forums and operates in a non-discriminatory manner with a focus on inclusion. Events are held in regular community venues and are either members only or open to all, depending upon the nature of the event. The project aims to empower its members, helping them to develop confidence and connections. Discriminatory practices frequently inhibited learning disabled people's sense of place within their community. The project aims to redress that balance by working alongside members and community resources to ensure disabled people are welcomed and have an opportunity to contribute. Cultural prejudices and disablist attitudes impact detrimentally on learning disabled people's rights to a sexual identity, and the project actively works to promote the legal rights of disabled people.

The case and practice examples outlined in this chapter illustrate that adopting a HRBA can provide a bridge between disparate agendas:

> In the current landscape of the integration of health and social care services a focus on human rights offers a common language and framework to help public bodies and their key partners stay focused on their key purpose – to improve people's lives (MWC and SHRC, 2015).

Scotland's mental health and capacity legislative framework has its foundations in a HRBA; however, for all the reasons detailed, the entire legislative framework for non-consensual care and treatment (AWI, MHA and ASP) requires to be comprehensively reviewed. When considering the legislative framework adopted, the MWC cautions:

> The starting point should not be to try to protect services from any possible legal challenge. It should be to devise a system which empowers people in care settings and protects them

---

77 Available from URL: www.dates-n-mates.co.uk (accessed 16 February 2018).
78 Available from URL: www.gov.scot/resource/0042/00424389.pdf (accessed 12 March 2018).

where necessary. It should focus not simply on capacity as a legal concept, but powerlessness as a lived experience (MWC, 2016).

The lack of judicial review in Scotland should not necessarily be regarded as a positive reflection on the functionality of the health and social care system. The previously cited cases, particularly those in England, have stimulated much healthy debate and deliberation about the human rights of disabled people. There is much that could be done to move away from a paternalistic approach to capacity and disability. Drawing up a formal supported decision-making framework, as illustrated in the Canadian example, may address some of the pressures on the guardianship system while providing safeguards to protect individuals from exploitation and abuse. The challenge is to design a system based upon a model of capacity that acknowledges a reliance on supports in the decision-making process. It should recognise 'that non-interference with liberty and autonomy does not necessitate neglect' (Glass, 1997, p. 30) or leaving disabled people to 'die with their rights on' (Treffert, 1987). It should also acknowledge that laws can have a pathologising effect in 'bureaucratising social relations and moral environments and so creating disruption in contexts previously regulated by extra-legal norms' (Cotterrell, 1992, p. 52).

Fundamentally, Scotland needs to rebalance its approach to disability and capacity considering anew its human rights obligations. The CRPD provides an opportunity to review, renew and refresh its approach to legal and mental capacity and disabled people– an issue, as this chapter has outlined, that is a source of significant contention in the field of health and social care.

Conclusion

Disabled people will not get access to full human and civil rights by being treated the same as non-disabled people. It is not enough to suggest that equality will be achieved by making the same resources available to all. In many situations, the human and civil rights of disabled people cannot be promoted without specific action being taken and resources being made available, which allow disabled people equal access. Many disabled people cannot access their right to a private and family life unless they have an entitlement to accessible housing, equipment and personal assistance (Morris, 2001, p. 11). The true transformative potential of the CRPD requires a far greater philosophical and cultural shift. It heralds a move from 'viewing people with disabilities as passive objects of treatment, management, charity and pity (and sometimes fear, abuse and neglect), towards a world view of people with disabilities as active subjects of human rights and dignity' (Lewis, 2010, p. 101). Providing appropriate supports for decision-making should enable a reduced reliance on substitute decision-making, so it is the exception rather than the rule in relation to people with impaired decision-making.

If Scotland can embrace the challenge, the CRPD has the potential to become a catalyst for the creation of a society based on greater equality and respect for diversity. It is reasonable and defensible to suggest that removing any discriminatory aspects of the law based upon physical, intellectual or psychosocial disability would ensure that all those who lack capacity, for whatever reason, would be treated according to the same principles. This is surely the basis for a fair, just and equitable capacity legislation.

Implementation of the full articulation of the CRPD also has the potential to shape the nation's views of citizenship and civic engagement. However, it is also wise to sound a note of caution. Despite its stated aims, the experience of the implementation of AWI legislation provides a salutary warning. The impact of any revised legislation lies in its implementation, how it will be interpreted and applied in practice. People with disabilities are among those who suffer most from the compliance gap between aspirational declarations and rights in reality. When formulating any new legislation and subsequent policy, it would be wise to be cognisant of the potential for unintended consequences. At a time of diminishing financial resources what, on the face of it, could be a laudable move to more informal supported decision-making may equally facilitate the State abrogating its responsibilities to support its citizens by transferring various risks to the individual (Gooding, 2015). Any revised system should have built-in safeguards to ensure that it does not abandon the most vulnerable in our society, to the preferences of those who support and care for them or to those who pay for their care and support.

The legislative framework within which we live and work as policymakers, practitioners, disabled people and their allies is crucial for setting out the landscape in which our lives are lived. There are, however, risks associated with recourse to the law; Richardson and Thorold (1999, p.

110) refer to the 'chilling effect of legalism' when discussing the limits of legal intervention and the law's ability to significantly influence behaviour. Attention needs to be paid to the risk that, when disabled people assert their right to take greater control over their own lives, this may result in 'rights based legalism'. This term describes the process whereby the locus of control of mentally or cognitively disabled people shifts from doctors to lawyers (Rose, 1985). The ECHR is a living instrument, and the findings of the ECtHR evolve and develop over time. The CRPD is a unique Convention, the participatory process by which it was created ensured that the voices, will and preferences of disabled people were writ large. It lays down a challenge to the nations of the world, and it is not not a challenge that should shirk.

The key lessons from this chapter are that 'for human rights to be meaningful, they are not about technical compliance with jurisprudence; they are about changing life on the ground' (Bartlett, 2014). International and national laws set the scene; however, the legal and practice case studies in this chapter illustrate that it is the implementation of policy in practice and the decisions that flow from that which make the difference to people's lives. The presence, or creation, of positive relationships and supports are crucial to human happiness and well-being. Adopting a HRBA and using the PANEL principles as a compass should help practitioners traverse the complex terrain of adult health and social care and ensure primacy of the will and preferences of disabled people.

CHAPTER 5

The Rights of Older Persons

> A society that does not value its older people denies its roots
> and endangers its future. Let us strive to enhance their capac-
> ity to support themselves for as long as possible and when they
> cannot do so anymore to care for them (President Mandela).[1]

Introduction

Historically, the international community has lacked a strong HRBA
to older persons. While existing human rights Conventions implic-
itly assume that human rights are for everyone, they very rarely cite
age explicitly as a reason why someone should not be discriminated
against. As a result, it is argued, age discrimination is often overlooked
on the international human rights stage (UN General Assembly, 2009).
This is not to suggest that issues affecting older persons have not been
researched and deliberated – more that such analysis has typically been
framed within 'medical, welfare, philosophical, political, economic' nar-
ratives rather than from a human rights perspective (Mégret, 2011, p.
38). However, recent years have witnessed emboldened advocacy calls
for improved international thinking and action on the human rights of
older persons. A wide range of stakeholders have campaigned for greater
visibility and increased use of international human rights standards to
address the challenges experienced by millions of older women and men
around the world.[2]

This chapter will briefly outline the international human rights
developments to date before going on to consider the national implications of human rights and older persons. This will be undertaken
by examining case law and practice examples pertinent to the field of

---

1 On announcing the International Year of Older Persons, 17 December 1998.
2 Available from URL: http://ageingcommitteegeneva.org (accessed 16 February 2018).

social care. The PANEL principles (of participation, accountability, non-discrimination, empowerment and legality) will be used throughout the chapter as a reflexive tool to aid analysis. First, however, consideration will be given to issues of language and definition as they relate to older persons.

Language and definition

The established language adopted by international human bodies refers to older persons, and this will be adopted throughout this chapter. Older persons are not a homogenous group, and the challenges they face in the protection or enjoyment of their human rights vary greatly. The Secretary General of the UN noted that 'older people are a heterogeneous group, encompassing both people who are major contributors to the development of society, as well as those who are in need of care and support' (UN General Assembly, 2009, p. 4). Mégret (2011, p. 45) highlights a definitional issue peculiar to older persons, termed the 'power/ vulnerability paradox', which recognises that, particularly in the West, representation of older persons is increasingly framed in terms of 'independence, prosperity and leisure'. The gap between the rich and poor has taken on a generational component with national news headlines focusing on the relative lack of opportunity afforded to younger people by comparison to the older generation.[3] Senior citizens concentrate a larger share of political power (ibid.), a situation reflected in the age configuration of the UK Westminster Parliament and the House of Lords. However, 'government by the elderly does not necessarily mean government for the elderly' (Mégret, p. 46). The paradox is that, while some older persons continue to lead active lives as part of their community, many others face homelessness, lack of adequate care or isolation. The flip side of the independent, wealthy older person's narrative is that of the looming 'problem' of a growing older population, characterised in terms of a 'demographic time bomb'.[4] Neither of these polar extreme

---

3 Available from URLs: www.dailymail.co.uk/news/article-2966649/Rise-rich-pensioner-65s-better-population-young-people-incomes-tumble.html (accessed 12 March 2018); www.savethestudent.org/news/report-shows-the-old-are-prospering-while-the-young-are-getting-poorer.html (accessed 12 March 2018); www.telegraph.co.uk/finance/personalfinance/11775373/Young-and-old-how-big-is-the-wealth-gap.html (accessed 16 February 2018); www.theguardian.com/commentisfree/2015/oct/24/young-bear-burden-of-pensioner-prosperity (accessed 16 February 2018).

4 Available from URLs: www.independent.co.uk/news/uk/politics/demographic-

depictions capture the more nuanced experience of older persons.

The supervisory body of the ICESCR,[5] the Committee on Economic, Social and Cultural Rights (CESCR), produced General Comment No. 6, which began by defining older people as those aged sixty and over.[6] This definition is important for clarification. The question of who should be perceived as an older person is more than just a function of chronological age (Miller, 2010); it also encompasses many other factors such as functional capacity, social involvement, and physical and mental health.[7] Intersectional discrimination is an essential component of any analysis of the experience of older persons, particularly when considering that age-related discrimination is often compounded by other forms of discrimination such as sex, socio-economic status, ethnicity or health status.[8] Regardless of their individual situation, it is critical that older persons not be marginalised, but rather brought into the mainstream of social and economic development (UN General Assembly, 2009, p. 4). This is particularly significant when we consider the changing make-up of the world's population and the impact this will have on social care policy and practice.

Demographics

The world's population is ageing. Increased life expectancy in conjunction with reduced fertility and declining birth rates are contributing to the changing balance of demographics. In developed regions of the world, the population aged sixty and over is expected to increase by more than 50% over the next four decades, rising from 264 million in 2009 to 416 million in 2050; while, in the developing world, the sixty and over population is projected to triple from 473 million in 2009 to 1.6 billion in 2050 (UN General Assembly, 2009, p. 3). The aged population are also getting older

---

time-bomb-government-woefully-underprepared-to-deal-with-britains-ageing-population-8533508.html (accessed 16 February 2018); www.theguardian.com/society/2004/jan/25/longtermcare.politics (accessed 16 February 2018); www.telegraph.co.uk/finance/economics/12068068/Mapped-how-a-demographic-time-bomb-will-transform-the-global-economy.html (accessed 16 February 2018).

5 ICESCR, 16 December 1966.

6 Committee on Economic, Social and Cultural Rights (1995) *General Comment No. 6, The Economic, Social and Cultural Rights of Older Persons* (Thirteenth Session, 1995), UN Doc. E/C.12/1995/16/Rev. 1.

7 See World Health Organization, 'Ageing and life course' (online). Available from URL: www.who.int/ageing/en (accessed 16 February 2018).

8 Available from URL: www.ohchr.org/EN/Issues/OlderPersons/Pages/OlderPersonsIndex.aspx (accessed 16 February 2018).

with those aged eighty and over to reach 395 million in 2050 (UNDESA, 2009). In 2050, for the first time in human history, there will be more persons aged over sixty than children in the world; more than one in five of the world's population will be aged sixty or older. Worldwide, women already outnumber men among those aged sixty or older, and are twice as numerous among those aged eighty or over (UN General Assembly, 2009, p. 3).

In the UK, there are now 11.8 million people aged sixty-five or over (ONS, 2017). Of those, over half a million are aged ninety and over, of which 70% are women (ONS, 2016a). The number of people aged sixty-five plus is projected to rise by more than 40% (40.77%) in the next seventeen years to more than 16 million (ONS, 2015). It is projected that, by 2040, nearly one in four people in the UK (24.2%) will be aged sixty-five or over (ONS, 2015). According to the Office for National Statistics (ONS), the UK's population is ageing more slowly than in other EU countries and by 2035 is predicted to be one of the least aged countries when compared to other European ones (ONS, 2012).

The 2011 census recorded a black and minority ethnic (BME) population of 211,000, or nearly 4% of the total population of Scotland. According to the same census, BME people account for less than 1% of all Scottish people aged over sixty (Wisdom in Practice, 2014a). Lesbian, gay, bisexual and transgender (LGBT) rights charity Stonewall estimates there are one million lesbian, gay and bisexual people aged over fifty-five in Britain (Stonewall, 2011). There may be around 100,000 LGBT people aged over fifty in Scotland, but estimates vary greatly. LGBT people aged over seventy have lived more than half of their adult lives in a Scotland where same-sex sexual activity was illegal, and this may have an impact on levels of self-disclosure (Wisdom in Practice, 2014b).

Approximately 3.64 million people in the UK aged sixty-five plus live alone, which equates to 32% of all people aged sixty-five plus in the UK and notably 70% of these are women (ONS, 2016a). Population projections for Scotland in 2037 suggest that, in most age groups up to seventy years old, men are more likely to live alone than women. From the age of seventy onwards, however, women are more likely to live alone, and this likelihood increases with age. This pattern reflects women's greater life expectancy, and the tendency of women to marry men who are older than them, which means that women are more likely to outlive their partners (NRS, 2014a).

In 2012, 96,400 men aged sixty-five or over were living alone; this is projected to nearly double (93% increase), to 186,100 in 2037. This compares to an increase of 33% in number of women aged sixty-five or over living alone, to 302,100.

The average gap in life expectancy between men and women is Scotland is projected to reduce (NRS, 2014b). The number of men aged eighty-five or over living alone is projected to more than treble, from 13,800 to 46,100, a 234% increase, compared to a 139% increase for women. Despite the sharper rise in the number of men living alone, there will still be many more women aged eighty-five or over living alone. In 2037, 108,000 women aged eighty-five or over (66% of women in this age group) are projected to live alone compared to 46,100 men (42% of men in this age group) (NRS, 2014a). This phenomenon has been identified as the 'feminization of ageing', where the numbers of older women eclipse that of older men; this also presents some major challenges for policymaking (UN General Assembly, 2009, p. 3). The shifting balance of demographics has implications for human rights, health and social care as will be identified when considering the legal and practice case studies later in this chapter.

Before moving on to consider the development of human rights in relation to older persons, it is important to offer a counter narrative to problematic framing of the increase in the older population. Worldwide, the unprecedented demographic changes illustrated in the statistics are a consequence of improved living standards and access to (even basic) healthcare systems. Declining fertility and birth rates are, in a part, a consequence of women gaining greater control over their reproductive rights, while greater longevity reflects the success of development efforts.[9] These developments should be celebrated, and the issues that flow from them better framed as those of social justice, dignity and rights.

The next challenge should be a focus on 'adding life to one's years rather than simply years to one's life' (UN General Assembly, 2009, p. 9) and the role that human rights and social care can play.

---

9   Committee on the Elimination of Discrimination against Women (CEDAW) (2010) 'General recommendation No. 27 on older women and protection of their rights' (online), CEDAW/C/2010/47/GC.1. Available from URL: http://reseau-crescendo.org/ cedawc201047gc-1-general-recommendation-n-27-on-older-women-and-protection-of-their-human-rights (accessed 16 February 2018).

The development of human rights and older persons

Article 25(1) of the 1948 Declaration of Human Rights states that:

> Everyone has the right to a standard of living adequate for the
> health and wellbeing of himself and his family, including food,
> clothing, housing and medical care and necessary social ser-
> vices, the right to security in the event of unemployment, sick-
> ness, disability, widowhood, old age or other lack of livelihood
> in circumstances beyond his control.[10]

Recognising the gendered aspect as a product of the era of its formation,
this statement represents the first reference to older persons in contem-
porary international human rights law. International obligations to older
persons are implicit in most core human rights treaties, such as the two
Covenants ICESCR[11] and ICCPR.[12] There is more explicit reference
in relation to CEDAW[13] and the CRPD.[14] However, explicit references
to older persons in binding international human rights instruments are
scarce. This notable absence of focus on the rights of older persons as a
distinct group began to be remedied only in the 1980s, with the International Plan on Ageing adopted by consensus of the 124 nations represented in the 1982 World Assembly on Ageing in Vienna ('Vienna
Plan').[15] This is regarded as the first international instrument on ageing to

---

10 Universal Declaration of Human Rights, Article 25(1), GA Res 217A (111), UN Doc.
A/810 at 71 (1948).

11 UN General Assembly, International Covenant on Economic, Social and Cultural Rights,
16 December 1966, United Nations.

12 UN General Assembly, International Covenant on Civil and Political Rights, 16 December
1966, United Nations.

13 The Convention on the Elimination of all Forms of Discrimination against Women, in
Article 11.1 includes reference to old age pertaining to the elimination of discrimination
against women's enjoyment of the right to social security. In 2010, CEDAW adopted
General Recommendation No. 27 on older women and their protection under the
convention. See: CEDAW (2010) 'General recommendation 27 on older women and
protection of their human rights' (online), CEDAW/C/2010/47/GC.1 (unedited
version). Available from URL: http://reseau-crescendo.org/cedawc201047gc-1-general-
recommendation-n-27-on-older-women-and-protection-of-their-human-rights (accessed
16 February 2018).

14 The CRPD includes reference to older people in Article 25(b) on health, and in Article 28
(2)(b) on an adequate standard of living and social protection, and there are additional
references to age-appropriate access to justice in Article 13 and age-sensitive measures of
protection in Article 16.

15 UN (1982) 'Vienna international plan of action' (online), Report of the World Assembly
on Ageing. Available from URL: www.un.org/development/desa/ageing/resources/
vienna-international-plan-of-action.html (accessed 16 February 2018).

offer guided thinking and the formulation of policies and programmes on ageing (Rodriguez-Pinzon and Martin, 2003). The 1991 United Nations Principles for Older Persons,[16] the 1992 Global Targets on Ageing for the Year 2001[17] and the 1992 'Proclamation on ageing'[18] further advanced international understanding of essential requirement for the well-being of older persons.[19]

The UN Principles on Older Persons are categorised as 'soft law'[20] and as such do not carry the same weight as a legally binding instrument. There is, however, a growing movement to have them turned into a Convention with accompanying reporting requirements. They also provide a positive influence on the development of domestic legislation, policy and practice: for example, in 2014 the Welsh government made the decision to embed these principles in its new Social Services and Well-being (Wales) Act, requiring all public bodies to have regard to them.[21]

The Madrid International Plan of Action on Ageing, 2002, adopted by the Second World Assembly on Ageing and endorsed by the UN General Assembly,[22] provided an international framework for dialogue, highlighting issues such as equal employment opportunities, social protection and social security, continued education and access

---

16 UN General Assembly (1991) 'Implementation of the International Plan of Action on ageing and related activities' (online), 74th plenary meeting, A/RES/46/91. Available from URL: www.un.org/documents/ga/res/46/a46r091.htm (accessed 16 February 2018). This document highlighted five focus areas as independence, participation, care, self-fulfilment and dignity.

17 UN General Assembly (1992a) 'Implementation of the International Plan of Action on ageing: Integration of older persons in development' (online), 89th plenary meeting, A/RES/47/86.

18 UN General Assembly (1992b) 'Proclamation on ageing' (online), 42nd plenary meeting, A/RES/47/5. Available from URL: www.un.org/documents/ga/res/47/a47r005.htm (accessed 16 February 2018).

19 UN General Assembly (2011) 'Summary of the Report of the Secretary-General to the Second World Assembly on Ageing' (online), A/66/173. Available from URL: www.ohchr.org/Documents/Issues/SForum/SForum2014/A.66.173_en.pdf (accessed 16 February 2018). The report is submitted pursuant to the General Assembly resolution 65/182 of December 2010. Approximately eighty written contributions were received for the preparation of this report, from member states, national human rights institutions, United Nations entities and non-governmental organizations, coalitions and other groups.

20 Soft law refers to rules that are neither strictly binding in nature nor completely lacking legal significance. In the context of international law, soft law refers to guidelines, policy declarations or codes of conduct which set standards of conduct. However, they are not directly enforceable.

21 Social Services and Well-being (Wales) Act 2014, s.7(1).

22 Resolution 57/167.

to healthcare.[23] The International Plan of Action includes the need to incorporate ageing into the global agenda with the goal to eliminate neglect, abuse and violence towards older people. It places primary responsibility on national governments, requiring that they develop and implement policies to ensure economic and social protection for older people, promoting and ensuring their good health, and making services and housing available and accessible. In December 2012, the UN General Assembly voted to mandate the Open-Ended Working Group on Ageing to draw up options for an international human rights instrument for older people, and mandated the UN Secretary General to compile a report of all existing legal instruments relating to the rights of older people.[24]

The ECtHR has, historically, produced scant jurisprudence on the human rights of older persons. This may flow from the relative silence of the European Convention and its Protocols on issues of rights for the older persons – in contrast to the 'European social charter' (see Article 23)[25] and the 'Charter on the fundamental rights of the European Union' (see Articles 21 and 25).[26] There are signs that this may be changing and that the court's legal analysis is beginning to mainstream the rights of older persons such as Article 2, the right to life in *Dodov v. Bulgaria*[27] and Article 6 Subsection 1, right to a fair trial in both *Dodov v. Bulgaria* and *X and Y v. Croatia*,[28] and Article 10, freedom of expression in *Heinisch v. Germany*.[29]

The *Heinisch v. Germany* case is worthy of some further consideration as, initially, it does not appear to be about the protection of older persons, focusing, as it does, on a whistle-blower's right to freedom of expression. It is an interesting judgement as it concerned the dismissal of a geriatric nurse after having brought a criminal complaint against her employer alleging deficiencies in the care provided. The applicant complained that her dismissal and the court's refusal to order

23 *supra* n. 19, p. 6.

24 General Assembly resolution 65/182 on 21 December 2010.

25 Council of Europe (1996) 'European social charter (revised)' (online), ETS 163. Available from URL: http://www.refworld.org/docid/3ae6b3678.html (accessed 16 February 2018).

26 European Union (2012) 'Charter of fundamental rights of the European Union' (online), 2012/C 326/02. Available from URL: http://eur-lex.europa.eu/legal-content/EN/TXT/?uri=CELEX%3A12012P%2FTXT (accessed 12 March 2018).

27 *Dodov v. Bulgaria* (App. No. 59548/00) [2008] ECHR (Fifth Section).

28 *X and Y v. Croatia* (App. No. 5193/09) [2011] ECHR.

29 *Heinisch v. Germany* (App. No. 28274/08) [2011] IRLR 922.

her reinstatement had violated Article 10 (freedom of expression) of the Convention. The court held that there had been a violation of Article 10 (freedom of expression) of the Convention, finding that the applicant's dismissal without notice had been disproportionate and that the domestic courts had failed to strike a fair balance between the need to protect the employer's reputation and the need to protect the applicant's right to freedom of expression. The court observed that, given the vulnerability of the older persons and the need to prevent abuse, the information disclosed had undeniably been of public interest,[30] stating:

> In societies with an ever growing part of their elderly population being subject to institutional care, and taking into account the particular vulnerability of the patients concerned, who often may not be in a position to draw attention to shortcomings in the care rendered on their own initiative, the dissemination of information about the quality or deficiencies of such care is of vital importance with a view to preventing abuse.[31]

Furthermore, the court ruled that public interest, in being informed about shortcomings in the provision of institutional care for older persons by a State-owned company, was so important that it outweighed the interest in protecting a company's business reputation and interests. The court appears to explicitly recognise the specific vulnerability of certain older persons, in this case those living in nursing homes. In doing so, it appears to identify vulnerability as a legitimate concept to inform the court's reasoning.[32] Importantly, the court expressed concern not only for the negative effect on the applicant's career, but also for the potential serious 'chilling effect' both on other company employees and on nursing-service employees generally. The consequence of this, it was considered, may discourage reporting in a sphere in which patients were frequently not capable of defending their own rights and where members of the nursing staff would be the first to become aware

---

30 ECtHR (2016) 'Elderly people and the European Convention on Human Rights' (online). Available from URL: www.echr.coe.int/Documents/FS_Elderly_ENG.pdf (accessed 16 February 2018).

31 *supra* n. 29, para 71.

32 Available from URL: https://strasbourgobservers.com/2011/09/05/mainstreaming-the-human-rights-of-older-persons (accessed 16 February 2018).

of shortcomings in the provision of care.[33] This judgement appears to explicitly recognise the additional vulnerability of older persons as a group requiring specific human rights protection.

In the UK, the ECHR finds expression through the Human Rights Act 1998 (HRA). The HRA provides a legal basis for some concepts fundamental to the well-being of older persons. For example, although dignity does not appear explicitly in the ECHR, the ECtHR has acknowledged that protection of dignity and human freedom is 'the very essence of the ECHR' and that protecting dignity is a matter of civilisation, *SW v. United Kingdom, CR v. United Kingdom* 1995.[34] According to Dupré (2009):

> human dignity has therefore emerged as an entirely judge-made concept with an uncertain normative basis and definition, generally located somewhere between the prohibition of torture and inhuman or degrading treatment (under Article 3, ECHR) and the right to privacy (Article 8, ECHR).[35]

The HRA now provides a legal framework that empowers older persons to demand that they be treated with respect for their dignity.[36] The ethics and values that underpin good practice in social care, such as autonomy, privacy and dignity, are at the core of human rights legislation. In this respect, among others, the HRA underpins health and social care policy and practice.

It is worth noting that, as with the other societal groups discussed in previous chapters, there is a distinct lack of case law in Scotland relating to older persons and social care. There is a growing body of case law from other UK courts on which to reflect, in order to demonstrate the role that human rights legislation has in defending or attempting to defend the rights of older persons in relation to matters of social care. Recognising the limitations of the law in affecting changes in behaviour, attention will also be paid to practice examples where the

---

33 *supra* n. 30.

34 *SW v.United Kingdom, CR v. United Kingdom* (1995) 21 EHRR 363.

35 Dupré, C. (2011) 'What does dignity mean in a legal context?' (online), *The Guardian*. Available from URL: www.theguardian.com/commentisfree/libertycentral/2011/mar/24/dignity-uk-europe-human-rights (accessed 16 February 2018).

36 Age UK (2012) 'The Human Rights Act and older people: An evidence paper' (online). Available from URL: www.ageuk.org.uk/globalassets/age-uk/documents/reports-and-publications/consultation-responses-and-submissions/equality-and-human-rights/csr_sept12_human_rights_policy.pdf (accessed 16 February 2018).

explicit adoption of a HRBA has improved the lives of older persons in the sphere of social care.

Before examining relevant legal cases and practice examples, it is worth noting the impact of the Equality Act 2010 on the lives of older persons. The Act makes it illegal for people to be treated less favourably because of their age, disability, gender, race, religion or belief and sexual orientation or transgender. It requires public bodies to fully consider the impact that changes in policy, such as the closure of a service, have on people with 'protected characteristics' such as disabilities. In addition, the Act continues the duty of service providers and employers to make 'reasonable adjustments' to ensure that people with disabilities are not disadvantaged.[37] Age discrimination that has a positive consequence may continue lawfully if it is 'objectively justifiable'. This includes, for example, interventions such as free flu vaccinations for people over the age of sixty-five.[38]

Social care case law and practice examples

The term 'social care for older persons' applies to a broad range of supports from relatively brief and infrequent home care style input to residential care support. It also includes support to older persons who undertake a caring role for others. Given the breadth of the area, legal cases for examination have been selected for their wider applicability or interest value.

Legal case: McDonald v. the United Kingdom[39]

The ECtHR decision concerns the right of a local authority to withdraw or amend care support where the recipient's circumstances are unchanged but where a cheaper alternative is available.

This case concerned Ms McDonald who was seventy-one years old. She had previously had a stroke and following a fall, in which she incurred a broken hip, her mobility was severely limited. Ms McDonald also experienced bladder problems that required that she use the toilet frequently at night. She was assessed as having an eligible need for support both during the day and 'assistance at night to use the commode'. Initially, Ms McDonald received overnight support. In 2008, the funding authority, as a cost-cutting measure, reduced the overnight support to four nights per week, on the basis that

---

37 Available from URL: www.equalityhumanrights.com/en/advice-and-guidance/age-discrimination (accessed 16 February 2018).

38 ibid., n. 280.

39 *McDonald v. the United Kingdom* [2014] ECHR 141.

her night-time toileting needs could be met by the provision of incontinence pads and absorbent sheets. The local authority subsequently assessed Ms McDonald as not requiring any overnight support. Ms McDonald claimed that the decision to reduce the funding for her support on the basis that she could use incontinence pads at night, even though she was not incontinent, amounted to a disproportionate and unjustifiable interference with her right to respect for private life, and undermined her dignity.

The ECtHR decided that, during the initial period, the reduction in Ms McDonald's support funding on the basis that she could use incontinence pads at night had interfered with her right to respect for her family and private life under Article 8 of the ECHR on the basis that it had not accorded with domestic law at the time. The court further declared inadmissible Ms McDonald's complaint concerning the latter period because the local authority (through assessment and subsequent care reviews) and the national courts (including the Court of Appeal and the Supreme Court) had balanced Ms McDonald's need for care with its wider responsibility for the well-being of the community. The State is afforded considerable discretion when it comes to decisions concerning the allocation of scarce resources and, as such, the interference with the Ms McDonald's rights had been 'necessary in a democratic society'.[40] This judgement provides an example of the exercise of the principle of proportionality[41] and the wide margin of appreciation the ECtHR affords States in relation to Article 8.[42]

To take her case to the ECtHR, Ms McDonald had to exhaust all domestic remedies. As an interesting adjunct to this, Lady Hale gave a dissenting judgement at the Supreme Court, stating:

> As Lord Lloyd put it in Barry: 'in every case, simple or complex, the need of the individual will be assessed against the standards of civilised society as we know them in the United Kingdom'.[43]
> In the UK, we do not oblige people who can control their bodily functions to behave as if they cannot do so, unless they themselves find this the more convenient course. We are, I still believe, a civilised society. I would have allowed this appeal.

---

40 Law Centre (NI) (2014) 'Human Rights and the provision of social care *McDonald v. the United Kingdom* (the McDonald case)' (online), Community Care Information Briefing 33. Available from URL: www.lawcentreni.org/Publications/Law-Centre-Information-Briefings/Community%20care%20briefings/CC-Briefing-33-Human-rights-and-social-care.pdf (accessed 16 February 2018).

41 The principle of proportionality requires that any decision taken by a public authority that affects a basic human right must be necessary, appropriate and reasonable.

42 The margin of appreciation is a concept developed by the ECtHR which allows it to take into consideration the fact that what the ECHR means in practice is interpreted differently in different member states. Under the margin of appreciation, judges in the ECtHR are obliged to take account of the cultural, historical and philosophical differences between the contracting state.

43 *R v. Gloucestershire County Council*, Ex p Barry [1997] AC 584.

Lady Hale's comments underline the position that the law is, at least in part, a reflection of the values of the society in which it operates. The ECHR is a 'living instrument' and the rights enshrined in the Convention must be interpreted in the light of present-day conditions to be practical and effective. Sociological, technological and scientific advances need to be taken account of as societal and cultural norms evolve. Issues that may have seemed unconscionable in the 1970s are unremarkable in the 2018. We need only look at the issue of gay marriage as an example of this process in action. The law, in part, reflects who and how we choose to be as a society, what compromises we believe should be expected of and tolerated by our fellow citizens, particularly those who are most vulnerable.

Ms McDonald's case highlights the importance for State-funding bodies – be that health or local authority – to identify and to give due consideration to human rights issues when making decisions concerning the provision of social care services in times of financial constraint. The PANEL principles again offer a useful tool for ensuring practitioners adopt a HRBA. Facilitating the full and meaningful participation of the individual in the assessment and ongoing review of their social care support needs is essential. Ensuring that these processes are recorded and are transparent and are shared would engender greater accountability. Taking into consideration necessary reasonable adjustments and ensuring a consciously non-discriminatory approach focused on the goals of independent living would ensure social care interventions are empowering and based on equality of opportunity. Critically, funders need to ensure the legality of any actions where they engage with the right to private life.

There have been many cases where residents of residential care homes have challenged local authority decisions to close the homes they reside in and move them to alternative accommodation. Generally, these decisions are financially driven and, as in the McDonald case, when challenged under ECHR Article 8, local authorities have been afforded significant latitude in respect of the balance of interests between the claimant and the wider community.[44]

---

44 R *(Wilson and others) v. Coventry City Council* [2008] EWHC 2300; R *(Rutter) v. Stockton on Tees Borough Council* [2008] EWHC 2651; R *(Turner and others) v. Southampton City Council* [2009] EWCA 1290; R *(on the application of Thomas) v. Havering London Borough Council: R (on the application of W) v. Coventry City Council* [2008] EWHC 2300.

Legal Case: R (on the application of Cowl and others) v. Plymouth City Council (2001)[45]

A local authority was considering closing a residential care home for older persons, for financial reasons. Several residents brought a case against the authority claiming that the closure of the home would be a breach of their human rights including their ECHR Article 8 right to respect for private life, family life and home. They argued that they had a reasonable expectation that the home would be their home for life. The case went to appeal and was found in their favour and the home was not closed, subject to further work being undertaken by the local authority.

Although the Court of Appeal found for the claimants, the court noted that the:

> ...importance of this appeal is that it illustrates that, even in disputes between public authorities and the members of the public for whom they are responsible, insufficient attention is paid to the paramount importance of avoiding litigation whenever this is possible.[46]

The court expressed concern regarding the protracted nature of the case and that recourse to the complaint procedure or mediation had not been pursued. Adopting an explicitly HRBA using the PANEL principles might have guided practitioners and residents through an alternative way of resolving the issues they faced. Focusing on the full and meaningful participation of residents in dialogue about the potential options might have averted such a lengthy and adversarial process. A concerted effort to ensure transparency and accountability might have ensured that the residents fully understood processes and procedures that local authority representatives had to follow to undertake an options appraisal. This might also, in turn, have enabled residents to engage more fully in the process. A non-discriminatory approach would have prompted analysis of the specific impact such a proposition might have on older persons and consideration of reasonable adjustments that may have ameliorated the impact. Thus potentially avoiding the situation where the appeal court had to direct the local authority to undertake assessment work to 'take into account the emotional, psychological and physical health of the residents and the impact of a move upon them.'[47]

---

45 *Frank Cowl v. Plymouth City Council* [2001] EWCA Civ 1935X.
46 ibid., n. 288, para 1.
47 *supra* n. 45, para 11(a).

The residents in this case were empowered to instruct a lawyer to challenge the decision of the local authority. It might have been more conducive to empower them in the whole process of decision-making around matters that affected their lives directly. Ultimately, the question of the legality of the action taken was tested in court, a time-consuming and expensive way of resolving matters of disagreement.

The PANEL principles work as both a proactive tool to improve practice and as a reflexive tool to consider whether policy and practice fulfil both the spirit and the letter of the law. As part of the implementation of the SNAP, the SHRC has developed an online catalogue of video case studies evidencing the impact of adopting a HRBA.[48] There is wealth of good practice in the field of social care support and older persons.

Practice Example: Scottish Care

Scottish Care is a representative body of the largest group of independent providers of health and social care across Scotland, delivering residential care, day care, care at home and housing support. The organisation embarked on a project to raise awareness of a HRBA, with the aim of drafting a 'Convention on the Rights of Residents in Care Homes for Adults and Older People'. Work was undertaken with residents and staff of care homes to identify what rights they believed needed to be promoted and protected to ensure that living in care is an empowering, dignified and fulfilling experience. A 'Convention' document made up of sixteen articles was compiled and launched.[49]

Commentators have noted a move away from collective rights for older persons as a group, towards more procedural rights for individuals (Higgs, 1997), a trend that has been exacerbated by a consumerist approach to personalisation. It is, however, possible to adopt a HRBA to community, as the next practice example illustrates.

Practice example: Life Changes Trust, Dementia Friendly Communities

---

In April 2015, the Life Changes Trust invested £3.4 million in fourteen dementia-friendly communities across Scotland, over a period of three years. The communities were selected on the basis they understood that people living with dementia and carers must be central to the development

---

48 Available from URL: www.scottishhumanrights.com/rights-in-practice/case-studies (accessed 16 February 2018).
49 ibid.

and growth of a dementia-friendly community. Almost all the communities have an intergenerational aspect to the work they do and a number have cultivated strong links with schools.

One example of such a collaboration was when local schoolchildren went to an allotment to work alongside residents of the local care home:

> The school teacher was the daughter of one of the care home residents... The allotment provided the opportunity for the teacher to introduce her dad (living with dementia) to her pupils, and the opportunity for a man living in a care home (her dad) to see his daughter at work as a teacher. For the children, it was an experience that gave them an insight into dementia, which could not be taught in a classroom (LCT, 2016a).

Practice Example: Charter of Rights for People with Dementia and their Carers, Scotland

---

The Cross-Party Group on Alzheimer's at the Scottish Parliament brings together Members of the Scottish Parliament with organisations representing the interests of people with dementia. Guided by a HRBA, the group produced a Charter of Rights[50] aimed at empowering people with dementia, those who support them and the community, to ensure their rights are recognised and respected.[51] Scotland's National Dementia Strategy (2010)[52] is built on The Charter of Rights for People with Dementia and their Carers in Scotland. Key to these developments has been the emphasis given to the involvement of people living with dementia and their carers. 'Promoting excellence: A framework for all health and social care staff working with people with dementia, their families and carers'[53] has been developed to ensure the implementation of the national strategy into practice at a personal, service provider and organisational level. A number of improvements to the implementation of the strategy have been suggested: such as a greater focus being given to data collection and reporting; recognition of the importance of transport and signage; increased emphasis on harnessing the potential of SDS; the explicit adoption of HRBA to palliative and end-of-life care for people with dementia; and an emphasis on the development of dementia-friendly communities (LCT, 2016b). The fact that Scotland has had a National Dementia Strategy since

---

50 Available from URL: www.gov.scot/Publications/2011/05/31085414/6 (accessed 16 February 2018).

51 Available from URL: http://careaboutrights.scottishhumanrights.com (accessed 16 February 2018).

52 Available from URL: www.gov.scot/Publications/2010/09/10151751/17 (accessed 16 February 2018).

53 Available from URL: www.gov.scot/resource/doc/350174/0117211.pdf (accessed 16 February 2018).

2010 demonstrates the clear commitment of the Scottish government to 'getting it right' for people living with dementia and their carers. By adopting a HRBA there is considerable potential to do more.

Conclusion

The implications of the demographic changes in relation to the growing number of older persons will place significant demands on health and social care services at a time when budgets are constrained. In this context, the question of how society chooses to respect, protect and fulfil the rights of older persons will become increasingly important. Older persons experience specific disadvantages and as such they are an identifiable group in terms of 'rights experience'. The legal and practice case examples highlighted in this chapter appear to illustrate that this growing population suffers violations that are 'at least' different in kind from those of other persons, making existing instruments and means of seeking protection and redress inadequate. International older persons' advocacy organisations suggest that none of the domestic and international efforts affords a comprehensive and group-tailored approach to the challenges faced by older persons (Mégret, 2011, p. 42).

The 'strategy of legality' argues that claims against human rights law violations become stronger when encapsulated in law (Chinkin, 2001). It, therefore, makes sense that there are increasing demands for the development of a Convention on the rights of older persons. There is a legitimate argument that the development of a dedicated international human rights treaty would reframe the older population from passive subjects to explicit rights holders with entitlements. It would require the State, policymakers and practitioners to actively work to respect, protect and fulfil the full suite of rights for older persons. While the future of a Convention on the rights of older persons is decided, it may be salient to acknowledge – as has been highlighted in previous chapters – the limitations of treaties or even domestic laws to effect change in practice on the ground and by extension the lived experience of those in receipt of social care support.

In the absence of a specifically tailored human rights Convention, the challenge must be to make most effective use of existing instruments and initiatives. Practitioners can use the PANEL principles as an everyday tool to guide human rights based practice. Older people and their friends and allies can use them to ensure their rights are being respected, protected and fulfilled. In this way, more can be done to build on the excellent examples of human rights based practice highlighted in this chapter – practices that are already making a real, positive and lasting difference to the experience of older persons accessing social care.

CHAPTER 6

Conclusion: The Way Forward

> **William Roper**: So, now you give the Devil the benefit of law!
>
> **Sir Thomas More**: Yes! What would you do? Cut a great road through the law to get after the Devil?
>
> **William Roper**: Yes, I'd cut down every law in England to do that!
>
> **Sir Thomas More**: Oh? And when the last law was down, and the Devil turned round on you, where would you hide, Roper, the laws all being flat? This country is planted thick with laws, from coast to coast, Man's laws, not God's! And if you cut them down, and you're just the man to do it, do you really think you could stand upright in the winds that would blow then? Yes, I'd give the Devil benefit of law, for my own safety's sake (Robert Bolt, *A Man for All Seasons*, 1960).

Human rights expressed through the UN Conventions, ECHR and the HRA provide an expression of the fundamental values of our society. They have the power to challenge and disrupt social orders based on exclusion and discrimination. They provide a powerful tool for the development of a culture based upon decency, respect and fairness for all. To capitalise on the transformational potential of human rights, it will be necessary to challenge the perception of human rights as the preserve of lawyers and academics. The focus needs to shift to human rights as an active tool of engaged citizenship.

The legal and practice case examples in the preceding chapters attest to the fact that litigation is important; it does, however, have distinct limitations, not least that the focus is on winning rather than solving societal problems and that 'the adversarial system does not necessarily reveal truth or yield justice' (Wolfensberger, 2013, p. 64). It also obscures the fact that human rights are not limited to the issue of protecting the individual interests of a claimant. They are also about achieving wider social goals (de Feyter, 2011, p. 37). For example, the HRA is much more than a tool for litigation – it was intended to provide 'a floor, rather than a ceiling', for human rights protection (Labour Party, 1997).[54] The UK Parliament wanted the legislation to contribute to the creation of 'a culture of respect for human rights', so that public services would be 'habitually and automatically responsive to human rights considerations in all their procedures and practices'.[55] It is this vision that underpins a HRBA to the design and delivery of social care services.

A HRBA, using the PANEL principles, can be used as both a proactive and a reflexive tool. It provides an ethical framework for those who use services to assess whether the supports they are receiving respect, protect and fulfil their human rights. It provides those working in social care with a way of ensuring the meaningful participation of those who access services. It offers a checking mechanism to assess whether, through their practices, they are accountable to those they serve. A HRBA requires proactive steps be taken to ensure nondiscriminatory practice, that consciously takes account of the multiple overlapping layers of discrimination and disadvantage that people experience. It provides a focus on engaging and empowering people who access services, which helps to cultivate high-quality services. A HRBA provides a set of common values, rooted in law, which can help those working in social care and those in receipt of services, when faced with the challenge of competing rights or interests (EHRC, 2013).

A HRBA does not have to replace other more traditional approaches to social care, such as those based on outcomes, social justice and citizenship. It offers the opportunity to enhance and contextualise these approaches with the solid backing of international human rights law. Rights-based practice enables frontline practitioners, families and those who use services to develop confidence that rights to security, dignity, privacy and economic opportunity are not charitable favours but are

---

54 Labour Party's 1997 election manifesto.

55 Lord Irvine, in oral evidence in response to Question 38, Joint Committee on Human Rights: implementation of the Human Rights Act 1998, Examination of witnesses, 19 March 2001. Available from URL: https://publications.parliament.uk/pa/jt200001/jtselect/jtrights/66/1031906.htm (accessed 16 February 2018).

instead internationally recognised and enforceable rights (Robson, 1997). It can guide the cultural change required to ensure that all those who access social care are, and are perceived to be, subjects with rights rather than objects of welfare (Dhanda, 2006). Indeed, local practice is essential to the development of the living ideals of human rights (Goodale, 2007) and is crucial for the cultivation of an ethics of social care.

Making rights real for every person in Scotland requires that the correct laws and institutions (structures) are in place to respect, protect and fulfil the full range of civil, political, economic, social and cultural rights. It needs effective means for putting these rights into practice (processes), through policy and strategy setting. However, this is not enough; these top-down approaches reinforce the view that human rights law is the preserve of lawyers and public servants rather than owned and exercised by the nation's citizenry. People need to see themselves as 'rights-holders' and have the confidence and resilience to assert their rights daily. The State should also see people as rights-holders. This can prevent the need to use the law, as problems are resolved at an early stage. The greater challenge, therefore, is in ensuring that the citizens of Scotland (and beyond) know and understand their human rights. That together as neighbours, friends, colleagues and professionals, they respect, protect and fulfil their human rights obligations. This can only be achieved if citizens are aware of their rights, that they own them and practise them in every arena of life.

The universality of human rights agreements can act as a common lexicon across national borders, cultures and faiths (or none) that facilitates engagement in dialogue about what unites rather than divides people. These everyday conversations, in the 'small places' such as the nursery, classroom, the GP clinic, at the kettle in the office or in the community centre, are what can bind rather than divide society and citizens. In this respect, effort needs to be given to nurturing the expressive, educational and proactive role of human rights (Fredman, 2008, p. 32). Every opportunity for engagement with a fellow citizen affords an opportunity to implement the PANEL principles and adopt a HRBA.

Practice Example

Alexander lived in a community-based service that sought to control him. He has a learning disability and mental health issues and had lived in institutional settings since the age of eight. He was fifty years old, unhappy and angry. He was subject to a Guardianship Order and a community-based Compulsory Treatment Order. He did not feel in control of any aspect of his life.

Adopting a HRBA, his support team started having different conversations with him:

Participation – 'How do you want to be supported, what would work for you?'

Accountability – 'We are here to support you to get the good life you want and we will work with you and others in your support network to make it happen.'

Non-discrimination – 'You have the same rights as others, the right to privacy in your home and to be treated with dignity and to be respected.'

Empowerment – 'What do you think would make the difference and let's work together to bring that about?'

Legality – 'The only restrictions that will be placed on you are ones that have legal sanction.'

The outcome was transformative. Within three years, Alexander had taken control of his life. He was no longer subject to any compulsory restrictive measures. He had met the love of his life, got married and moved into their marital home. He continues to need a low level of support, mainly with managing his finances. He is flourishing.

For practitioners, adopting a HRBA to their practice within social care could be similarly transformational. That is not to suggest that respecting a person's human rights will automatically guarantee them having a good life. Some of the things that make life better can neither be bought nor legislated, but must be freely given by fellow citizens: for example, friendship, neighbourliness, love and compassion. Respecting, protecting and promoting human rights ensures the provision of a set of conditions that, if not realised, may result in detriment. Put quite simply, human rights are intended to ensure that individuals have the essential equipment they need to have a chance at happiness.

This book contains many inspiring examples of the transformative potential of adopting a HRBA to social care practice. In doing so, it is hoped that it fulfils its purpose of adding another branch to Eleanor Roosevelt's 'curious grapevine'.

APPENDIX 1

European Convention on Human Rights

ARTICLE 1: *Obligation to respect human rights*

The High Contracting Parties shall secure to everyone within their jurisdiction the rights and freedoms defined in Section I of this Convention.

SECTION I RIGHTS AND FREEDOMS

ARTICLE 2: *Right to life*

1. Everyone's right to life shall be protected by law. No one shall be deprived of his life intentionally save in the execution of a sentence of a court following his conviction of a crime for which this penalty is provided by law.

2. Deprivation of life shall not be regarded as inflicted in contravention of this Article when it results from the use of force which is no more than absolutely necessary:

(a) in defence of any person from unlawful violence;

(b) in order to effect a lawful arrest or to prevent the escape of a person lawfully detained;

(c) in action lawfully taken for the purpose of quelling a riot or insurrection.

ARTICLE 3: *Prohibition of torture*

No one shall be subjected to torture or to inhuman or degrading treatment or punishment.

ARTICLE 4: *Prohibition of slavery and forced labour*

1. No one shall be held in slavery or servitude.

2. No one shall be required to perform forced or compulsory labour.

3. For the purpose of this Article the term 'forced or compulsory labour' shall not include:

(a) any work required to be done in the ordinary course of detention imposed according to the provisions of Article 5 of this Convention or during conditional release from such detention;

(b) any service of a military character or, in case of conscientious objectors in countries where they are recognised, service exacted instead of compulsory military service;

(c) any service exacted in case of an emergency or calamity threatening the life or well-being of the community;

(d) any work or service which forms part of normal civic obligations.

ARTICLE 5: *Right to liberty and security*

1. Everyone has the right to liberty and security of person. No one shall be deprived of his liberty save in the following cases and in accordance with a procedure prescribed by law:

(a) the lawful detention of a person after conviction by a competent court;

(b) the lawful arrest or detention of a person for non-compliance with the lawful order of a court or in order to secure the fulfilment of any obligation prescribed by law;

(c) the lawful arrest or detention of a person effected for the purpose of bringing him before the competent legal authority on reasonable suspicion of having committed an offence or when it is reasonably considered necessary to prevent his committing an offence or fleeing after having done so;

(d) the detention of a minor by lawful order for the purpose of educational supervision or his lawful detention for the purpose of bringing him before the competent legal authority;

(e) the lawful detention of persons for the prevention of the spreading of infectious diseases, of persons of unsound mind, alcoholics or drug addicts or vagrants;

(f) the lawful arrest or detention of a person to prevent his effecting an unauthorised entry into the country or of a person against whom action is being taken with a view to deportation or extradition.

2. Everyone who is arrested shall be informed promptly, in a language which he understands, of the reasons for his arrest and of any charge against him.

3. Everyone arrested or detained in accordance with the provisions of paragraph 1(c) of this Article shall be brought promptly before a judge or other officer authorised by law to exercise judicial power and shall be entitled to trial within a reasonable time or to release pending trial. Release may be conditioned by guarantees to appear for trial.

4. Everyone who is deprived of his liberty by arrest or detention shall be entitled to take proceedings by which the lawfulness of his detention shall be decided speedily by a court and his release ordered if the detention is not lawful.

5. Everyone who has been the victim of arrest or detention in contravention of the provisions of this Article shall have an enforceable right to compensation.

ARTICLE 6: Right to a fair trial

1. In the determination of his civil rights and obligations or of any criminal charge against him, everyone is entitled to a fair and public hearing within a reasonable time by an independent and impartial tribunal established by law. Judgement shall be pronounced publicly but the press and public may be excluded from all or part of the trial in the interests of morals, public order or national security in a democratic society, where the interests of juveniles or the protection of the private life of the parties so require, or to the extent strictly necessary in the opinion of the court in special circumstances where publicity would prejudice the interests of justice.

2. Everyone charged with a criminal offence shall be presumed innocent until proved guilty according to law.

3. Everyone charged with a criminal offence has the following minimum rights:

(a) to be informed promptly, in a language which he understands and in detail, of the nature and cause of the accusation against him;

(b) to have adequate time and facilities for the preparation of his defence;

(c) to defend himself in person or through legal assistance of his own choosing or, if he has not sufficient means to pay for legal assistance, to be given it free when the interests of justice so require;

(d) to examine or have examined witnesses against him and to obtain the attendance and examination of witnesses on his behalf under the same conditions as witnesses against him;

(e) to have the free assistance of an interpreter if he cannot understand or speak the language used in court.

ARTICLE 7: *No punishment without law*

1. No one shall be held guilty of any criminal offence on account of any act or omission which did not constitute a criminal offence under national or international law at the time when it was committed. Nor shall a heavier penalty be imposed than the one that was applicable at the time the criminal offence was committed.

2. This Article shall not prejudice the trial and punishment of any person for any act or omission which, at the time when it was committed, was criminal according to the general principles of law recognised by civilised nations.

ARTICLE 8: *Right to respect for private and family life*

1. Everyone has the right to respect for his private and family life, his home and his correspondence.

2. There shall be no interference by a public authority with the exercise of this right except such as is in accordance with the law and is necessary in a democratic society in the interests of national security, public safety or the economic well-being of the country, for the prevention of disorder or crime, for the protection of health or morals, or for the protection of the rights and freedoms of others.

ARTICLE 9: *Freedom of thought, conscience and religion*

1. Everyone has the right to freedom of thought, conscience and religion; this right includes freedom to change his religion or belief and freedom, either alone or in community with others and in public or private, to manifest his religion or belief, in worship, teaching, practice and observance.

2. Freedom to manifest one's religion or beliefs shall be subject only to such limitations as are prescribed by law and are necessary in a democratic society in the interests of public safety, for the protection of public order, health or morals or for the protection of the rights and freedoms of others.

ARTICLE 10: Freedom of expression

1. Everyone has the right to freedom of expression. This right shall include freedom to hold opinions and to receive and impart information and ideas without interference by public authority and regardless of frontiers. This Article shall not prevent States from requiring the licensing of broadcasting, television or cinema enterprises.

2. The exercise of these freedoms, since it carries with it duties and responsibilities, may be subject to such formalities, conditions, restrictions or penalties as are prescribed by law and are necessary in a democratic society, in the interests of national security, territorial integrity or public safety, for the prevention of disorder or crime, for the protection of health or morals, for the protection of the reputation or rights of others, for preventing the disclosure of information received in confidence, or for maintaining the authority and impartiality of the judiciary.

ARTICLE 11: Freedom of assembly and association

1. Everyone has the right to freedom of peaceful assembly and to freedom of association with others, including the right to form and to join trade unions for the protection of his interests.

2. No restrictions shall be placed on the exercise of these rights other than such as are prescribed by law and are necessary in a democratic society in the interests of national security or public safety, for the prevention of disorder or crime, for the protection of health or morals or for the protection of the rights and freedoms of others. This Article shall not prevent the imposition of lawful restrictions on the exercise of these rights by members of the armed forces, of the police or of the administration of the State.

ARTICLE 12: Right to marry

Men and women of marriageable age have the right to marry and to found a family, according to the national laws governing the exercise of this right.

ARTICLE 13: Right to an effective remedy

Everyone whose rights and freedoms as set forth in this Convention are violated shall have an effective remedy before a national authority notwithstanding that the violation has been committed by persons acting in an official capacity.

ARTICLE 14: Prohibition of discrimination

The enjoyment of the rights and freedoms set forth in this Convention shall be secured without discrimination on any ground such as sex, race, colour, language, religion, political or other opinion, national or social origin, association with a national minority, property, birth or other status.

ARTICLE 15: Derogation in time of emergency

1. In time of war or other public emergency threatening the life of the nation any High Contracting Party may take measures derogating from its obligations under this Convention to the extent strictly required by the exigencies of the situation, provided that such measures are not inconsistent with its other obligations under international law.

2. No derogation from Article 2, except in respect of deaths resulting from lawful acts of war, or from Articles 3, 4 (paragraph 1) and 7 shall be made under this provision.

3. Any High Contracting Party availing itself of this right of derogation shall keep the Secretary General of the Council of Europe fully informed of the measures which it has taken and the reasons therefor. It shall also inform the Secretary General of the Council of Europe when such measures have ceased to operate and the provisions of the Convention are again being fully executed.

ARTICLE 16: Restrictions on political activity of aliens

Nothing in Articles 10, 11 and 14 shall be regarded as preventing the High Contracting Parties from imposing restrictions on the political activity of aliens.

ARTICLE 17: Prohibition of abuse of rights

Nothing in this Convention may be interpreted as implying for any State, group or person any right to engage in any activity or perform any act aimed at the destruction of any of the rights and freedoms set forth herein or at their limitation to a greater extent than is provided for in the Convention.

ARTICLE 18: Limitation on use of restrictions on rights

The restrictions permitted under this Convention to the said rights and freedoms shall not be applied for any purpose other than those for which they have been prescribed.

APPENDIX 2

UK Human Rights Commitments

Figure A.1: Summary of Articles 19–59 (Finch and McGroarty, 2014)

Section	Protocols
Section 2 Articles 19–51 Establishment of the European Court of Human Rights	Protocols 11, 14 Restructuring the organisation Amending procedures
Section 3 Articles 52–59 Miscellaneous provisions, including procedures for reservations, ratification and derogation	Protocols 2, 3, 5, 8, 9, 10 *(All now defunct – included in the main Articles of Protocol 11)*

Figure A.2: Status of Protocols in the UK (Finch and McGroarty, 2014)

Protocol		UK status
1	1 Right to peaceful enjoyment of possessions 2 Right to Education 3 Right to free elections	Ratified Ratified (reservation) Ratified
4	1 Prohibition of imprisonment for debt 2 Freedom of movement 3 Prohibition of expulsion of nationals 4 Prohibition of collective expulsion of aliens	Signed Signed Signed Signed
6	Abolition of the death penalty	Ratified
7	1 Procedural safeguards relating to the expulsion of aliens 2 Right of appeal in criminal matters 3 Compensation for wrongful conviction 4 Right not to be tried or punished twice 5 Equality between spouses	Not signed Not signed Not signed Not signed Not signed
11	Restructuring the organisation	Ratified
12	General prohibition of discrimination	Not signed
13	Complete abolition of the death penalty	Ratified
14	Amendments to the control system of the Convention	Ratified

REFERENCES

Age UK (2012) 'The Human Rights Act and older people: An evidence paper' (online). Available from URL: www.ageuk.org.uk/globalassets/age-uk/documents/reports-and-publications/consultation-responses-and-submissions/equality-and-human-rights/csr_sept12_human_rights_policy.pdf (accessed 16 February 2018)

Alston, P. and Goodman, R. (2012) *International Human Rights*, Oxford: University Press

Audit Scotland (2012) *Commissioning Social Care*, Edinburgh: Audit Scotland

Audit Scotland (2014) *Self-Directed Support*, Edinburgh: Audit Scotland

Audit Scotland (2016) *Social Work in Scotland*, Edinburgh: Audit Scotland

Audit Scotland (2017) *Self-Directed Support: 2017 Progress Report*, Edinburgh: Audit Scotland

Bach, M. and Kerzner, L. (2010) *A New Paradigm for Protecting Autonomy and the Right to Legal Capacity*, Ontario, Canada: Law Commission of Ontario

Barnes, C. (1996) 'Theories of disability and the origins of the oppression of disabled people in western society', in Barton, L. (ed.) (1996) *Disability and Society: Emerging Issues and Insights*, Harlow: Addison Wesley Longman, pp. 43–60

Barnes, C. and Mercer, G. (2006) *Independent Futures: Creating User-Led Disability Services in a Disabling Society*, Bristol: Policy Press, pp. 317–20

Bartlett, P. (2014) 'Reforming the Deprivation of Liberty Safeguards (DOLS): what is it exactly that we want?', *European Journal of Current Legal Issues*, Vol. 20, No. 3, pp. 4–22

Bauer, J. A. (1999) *The East Asian Challenge for Human Rights*, Cambridge: Cambridge University Press

Beauchamp, T. and Childress, J. (1994) *Principles of Biomedical Ethics* (4th edn), New York, NY: Oxford University Press

Bogdanor, V. (2009) *The Human Rights Act: Cornerstone of the New Constitution*, in *The New British Constitution*, Oxford: Hart

Brownlie, I. and Goodwin-Gill, G. S. (2010) *Brownlie's Documents on Human Rights*, Oxford: Oxford University Press

Bunch, C. (1992) 'Violence against women is a violation of human rights', *WILDAF (Women in Law and Development in Africa) News*, Vol. 4

Cantwell, N. (1992) 'The origins, development and significance of the UNCRC', in Detrick, S. (1992) *The UNCRC: A Guide to the Travaux Preparatoires*, Rotterdam: Springer Netherlands

Carers UK (2012) *Sandwich Caring: Combining Childcare with Caring for Older or Disabled Relatives*, London: Carers UK

Carers UK (2015) *Valuing Carers 2015: The Rising Value of Carers' Support*,

London: Carers UK

Carver, R. (2010) 'A new answer to an old question: national human rights institutions and the domestication of international law', *Human Rights Law Review*, Vol. 10, No. 1, pp. 1–32

Centre for Women and Democracy (2015) *Sex and Power 2013: Who Runs Britain?*, London: Counting Women In Coalition

Charlesworth, H. and Chinkin, C. (2000) *The Boundaries of International Law: A Feminist Analysis*, Manchester: Manchester University Press, p. 33

Charlesworth, H., Chinkin, C. and Wright, S. (1991) 'Feminist approaches to international law', *American Journal of International Law*, Vol. 85

Chetty, K. D. (2012) *Personalisation and Human Rights: A Discussion Paper*, Edinburgh: SHRC, Neighbourhood Networks, Alzheimers Scotland and the Centre for Welfare Reform

Chetty, K., Dalrymple, J. and Simmons, H. (2012) *Personalisation and Human Rights: A Discussion Paper*, Sheffield: Centre for Welfare Reform

Chinkin, C. (2001) 'Human rights and the politics of representation: is there a role for international law?', in Byers, M. (2001) *The Role of Law in International Politics: Essays in International Relations and International Law*, Oxford: Oxford University Press, pp. 131–48

Christie Commission (2011) *Commission on the Future Delivery of Public Services*, Edinburgh: Scottish Government

Coggon, J. and Miola, J. (2011) 'Autonomy, liberty and medical decision-making', *The Cambridge Law Journal*, Vol. 70, No. 3, pp. 523–47

Commissioner for Human Rights (2012) *The Rights of People with Disabilities to Live Independently and Be Included in the Community*, Strasbourg: Council of Europe Publishing

Committee on the Elimination of Discrimination against Women (CEDAW) (2010) 'General recommendation No. 27 on older women and protection of their rights' (online), CEDAW/C/2010/47/GC.1. Available from URL: http://reseau-crescendo.org/cedawc201047gc-1-general-recommendation-n-27-on-older-women-and-protection-of-their-human-rights (accessed 16 February 2018)

Connolly, M. A. (2008) *Morals, Rights and Practice in the Human Services*, London: Jessica Kingsley Press

Connors, J. (1989) *Violence Against Women in the Family*, New York: United Nations

Cotterrell, R. (1992) *The Sociology of Law*, London: Butterworths

Cracknell, R. (2012) *Women in Public Life, the Professions and the Boardroom*, London: House of Commons Library

Crenshaw, K. (1989) 'Demarginalizing the intersection of race and sex: A black feminist critique of antidiscrimination doctrine, feminist theory and antiracist politics', *University of Chicago Legal Forum*, Vol. 1, pp. 139–67

Crowther, N. (2017) 'After the UN CRPD examination – what now?' (online). Available from URL: https://makingrightsmakesense.wordpress.com/2017/09/05/after-the-uncrpd-examination-what-now (accessed 15 February 2018)

de Feyter, K. (2011) 'Sites of rights resistence', in *The Local Relevance of Human*

Rights, Cambridge: Cambridge University Press, pp. 11–39

de Feyter, K. and Parmentier, S. (2011) 'Introduction: Reconsidering human rights from below', in de Feyter, K. (2011) *The Local Relevance of Human Rights*, Cambridge: Cambridge University Press, pp. 1–10

Dhanda, A. (2006) Legal capacity in the disability rights convention: Stranglehold of the past or lodestar for the future, *Syracuse Journal of International Law and Commerce*, Vol. 34, p. 429

Dicey, A. V. (1959) *Introduction to the Study of Law and the Constitution* (10th edn) London: Macmillan

Donnelly, J. (2003) *Universal Human Rights in Theory and Practice*, Ithaca, NY: Cornell University Press

Drake, R. (1999) *Understanding Disability Politics*, London: Macmillan Press

Dupré, C. (2011) 'What does dignity mean in a legal context?' (online), *The Guardian*. www.theguardian.com/commentisfree/libertycentral/2011/mar/24/dignity-uk-europe-human-rights (accessed 16 February 2018)

EHRC (2010) *Significant Inequalities in Scotland: Identifying Significant Inequalities and Priorities for Action*, Glasgow: Equality and Human Rights Commission

EHRC (2011) *Hidden in Plain Sight: Inquiry into Disability Related Harassment*, Glasgow: Equality and Human Rights Commission

EHRC (2013) *Guidance on Human Rights for Commissioners of Home Care*, Manchester: Equality and Human Rights Commission

EHRC (2014a) 'Concluding observations of the Committee on the Elimination of Discrimination Against Women' (online). Available from URL: www.equalityhumanrights.com/sites/default/files/cedaw_concluding_observations_251114_1.pdf (accessed 12 March 2018)

EHRC (2014b) *Cumulative Impact Assessment, Research Report 94*, London: Equality and Human Rights Commission

Elsley, S., Backettt-Milburn, K. and Jamieson, L. (2007) *Review of Research on Vulnerable Young People and Their Transitions to Independent Living*, Edinburgh: Centre for Research on Families and Relationships, University of Edinburgh

Engender (2015) *Welfare Reform Committee Debate on Women and Social Security*, Edinburgh: Engender

Engender (2017) *Sex and Power in Scotland*, Edinburgh: Engender

Ewing, K. D. (1999) 'The Human Rights Act and parliamentary democracy', *The Modern Law Review*, Vol. 62, No. 1, pp. 79–99

Fennell, P. W. H. and Khaliq, U. (2011) 'Conflicting or complementary obligations? The UN Disability Rights Convention, the European Convention on Human Rights and English law', *European Human Rights Law Review*, Vol. 6, pp. 662–74

Finch, V. and McGroarty, J. (2014) *Human Rights Law Essentials*, Edinburgh: Edinburgh University Press

Finkelstein, V. (1991) 'Disability: An administrative challenge?', in Oliver, M. (1991) *Social Work: Disabled People and Disabling Environments*, London: Jessica Kingsley, pp. 19–39

Finkelstein, V. (2001) 'The social model of disability repossessed' (online), Manchester Coalition of Disabled People. Available from URL: http://disability-studies.leeds.ac.uk/files/library/finkelstein-soc-mod-repossessed.pdf

(accessed 12 March 2018)

FRA (2014) *Violence Against Women: An EU-Wide Survey*, Vienna: European Union Agency for Fundamental Rights

Fredman, S. (2008) *Human Rights Transformed: Positive Rights and Positive Duties*, Oxford: Oxford University Press

Fredman, S. (2013) 'The CEDAW in the UK', in Hellum, A. and Aasen, H. (2013) *Women's Human Rights: CEDAW in International, Regional and National Law, Studies on Human Rights Conventions*, Cambridge: Cambridge University Press, pp. 511–30

Freeman, M. (2000) 'The future of children's rights', Children and Society, Vol. 14, No. 4, pp. 277–93

Freeman, M. (2002) *Human Rights*, Cambridge: Polity Press

Glass, K. (1997) 'Refining definitions and devising instruments: Two decades of assessing mental competence', *International Journal of Law and Psychiatry*, Vol. 20, No. 1, p. 30

Goodale, M. A. (2007) *The Local Practice of Human Rights: Tracking Law Between the Global and the Local*, Cambridge: Cambridge University Press

Gooding, P. (2013) 'Supported decision-making: A rights-based disability concept and its implications for mental health law', *Psychiatry, Psychology and Law*, Vol. 20, No. 3, pp. 431–51

Gooding, P. (2015) 'Navigating the "flashing amber lights" of the right to legal capacity in the United Nations Convention on the Rights of Persons with Disabilities: Responding to major concerns', *Human Rights Law Review*, Vol. 15, No. 1, pp. 45–71

Goodley, D., Lawthom, R. and Runswick-Cole, K. (2014) 'Dis/ability and austerity: Beyond work and slow death', *Disability and Society*, Vol. 29, No. 6, pp. 980–4

Grant, J. P. and Sutherland, E. E. (2009) 'International standards and Scots law', in Cleland, A. and Sutherland, E. (2009) *Children's Rights in Scotland*, Edinburgh: W. Green

Grdinic, E. (1999) 'Application of the elements of torture and other forms of ill-treatment, as defined by the European Court and Commission of Human Rights, to the incidents of domestic violence', *Hastings International and Comparative Law Review*, Vol. 23, p. 217

Hare, I. (2004) 'Defining social work for the 21st century: The International Federation of Social Workers' revised definition of social work', *International Social Work*, pp. 407–24

Harris, P. (1995) 'Who am I? Concepts of disability and their implications for people with learning difficulties', *Disability and Society*, Vol. 10, pp. 341–51

Heydon, J. (2014) 'Are bills of rights necessary in common law systems?', *Law Quarterly Review*, pp. 392–412

Higgs, P. (1997) 'Citizenship theory and old age: Social rights to surveillance', in Jamieson, A., Harper, S. and Victor, C. (1997) *Critical Approaches to Ageing and Later Life*, Buckingham: Open University Press

Hollomotz, A. (2009) ' "May we please have sex tonight?": People with learning difficulties pursuing privacy in residential group settings', *British Journal of Learning Disabilities*, Vol. 37, pp. 91–7

Hopkins, C. (2001) 'Rescripting relationships: Towards a nuanced theory of intimate violence as sex discrimination', *Virginia Journal of Social Policy and the Law*, Vol. 9, pp. 411–69

House of Lords, House of Commons Joint Committee on Human Rights (2011) *Legislative Scrutiny: Welfare Reform Bill*, London: The Stationery Office

Human Rights Futures Project (2011) *Protection of Children's Rights under the Human Rights Act 1998: Legal Briefing*, London: London School of Economics

Hunt, P. (1981) 'Settling accounts with the parasite people: A critique of "A Life Apart" by E. J. Miller and G. V. Gwynne', in UPIAS (1981) *Disability Challenge (1)*, London: Union of the Physically Impaired Against Segregation, pp. 37–50

Ife, J. (2012) *Human Rights and Social Work: Towards Rights-Based Practice*, Cambridge: Cambridge University Press

IFS (2011) *The Impact of Tax and Benefit Reforms by Sex: Some Simple Analysis*, London: Institute for Fiscal Studies. Available from URL: www.ifs.org.uk/publications/5610 (accessed 15 February 2018)

Ipsos MORI (2009) *The Case for Change: Why England Needs a New Care and Support System. Engagement Findings*, London: Central Office of Information

Ipsos MORI (2011) 'Public opinion research on social care funding: A literature review on behalf of the Commission on the Funding of Care and Support', in *Fairer Care Funding: Supporting Documents*, London: HM Government

Ishay, M. (2004) 'What are human rights? Six historical controversies', *Journal of Human Rights*, Vol. 3, No. 3, pp. 359–71

Johnson, D. (1992) 'Cultural and regional pluralism in the drafting of the UNCRC', in Freeman, M. and Veerman, P. (1992) *The Ideologies of Children's Rights*, Dordrecht: Brill, pp. 95–114

Johnstone, R. (2006) 'Feminist influence in the United Nations Human Rights Treaty bodies', *Human Rights Quarterly*, Vol. 28, pp. 148–85

Kavanagh, A. (2004) 'The elusive divide between interpretation and legislation under the Human Rights Act 1998', *Oxford Journal of Legal Studies*, Vol. 24, No. 2, pp. 259–85

Keene, A. and Ward, A. D. (2016) ' "With and without best interests": The Mental Capacity Act 2005, the Adult with Incapacity (Scotland) Act 2000 and constructing decisions', *International Journal of Mental Health and Capacity Law*, Vol. 22, pp. 17–37

Kennedy, D. (2004) *The Dark Side of Virtue: International Humanitarianism Reassessed*, Princeton: Princeton University Press

Kerzner, L. (2011) 'Paving the way to full realization of the CRPD's right to legal capacity and supported decision-making: A Canadian perspective', *In from the Margins: New Foundations for Personhood and Legal Capacity in the 21st Century*, Vancouver, BC: Peter Wall Institute for Advanced Studies, University of British Columbia

Kilkelly, U. (2015) 'The CRC in litigation under the ECHR', in Liefaard, T. and Doek, J. (2015) *Litigating the Rights of the Child*, Dordrecht: Springer, pp. 193–210

Kong, C. (2015) 'The Convention for the Rights of Persons with Disabilities and Article 12: Prospective feminist lessons against the "will and preferences" paradigm', *Laws*, Vol. 4, No. 4, p. 709

Kumar, C. R.(2006) 'National human rights institutions (NHRIs) and economic, social and cultural rights: Towards the institutionalization and developmentalization of human rights', *Human Rights Quarterly*, Vol. 28, No. 3, pp. 755–79

Labour Party (1997) *Election Manifesto*, London: Labour Party

Law Society of Scotland (2012) *Response to Office of the Public Guardian (Scotland) Paper, Early Deliberations on Graded Guardianship, 2011*, Edinburgh: Law Society of Scotland

LCT (2016a) *Dementia Friendly Communities in Scotland, Report 2 – The First Year April 2015*, Glasgow: Life Changes Trust

LCT (2016b) *Scotland's Third National Dementia Strategy, Response to the Dementia Dialogue 2015/16*, Glasgow: Life Changes Trust

Learning Disability Alliance Scotland (2010) *Stuck – 869 People with Learning Disabilities Resident in Care Homes for Older People in Scotland*, Dalkeith: Learning Disability Alliance Scotland

Lewis, O. (2010) 'The expressive, educational and proactive roles of human rights: An analysis of the United Nations Convention on the Rights of Persons with Disabilities', in McSherry, B. and Weller, P. (2010) *Rethinking Rights Based Mental Health*, Sydney, NSW: Hart Publishing, pp. 97–128

LGA (2013) *The Local Impacts of Welfare Reform: An Assessment of Cumulative Impacts and Mitigations*, London: Local Government Association

Llewellyn, A. and Hogan, K. (2000) 'The use and abuse of models of disability', *Disability and Society*, Vol. 15, No. 1, pp. 157–65

McKay, C. (2015) *Substituted Decision Making, Deprivation of Liberty and Human Rights*, Edinburgh: Mental Welfare Commission for Scotland

Mackenzie, C. and Stoljar, N. (2000) *Relational Autonomy: Feminist Essays on Autonomy, Agency and the Social Self*, New York, NY: Oxford University

McQuigg, R. (2011) *International Human Rights Law and Domestic Violence: The Effectiveness of International Human Rights Law*, London: Taylor and Francis

Marshall, J. (2003) *Children and Poverty. Some Questions Answered. Briefing 1*, London: Childhood Poverty Research and Policy Centre (CHIP)

Marshall, K. (2009) 'The history and philosophy of children's rights in Scotland', in Cleland, A. and Sutherland, E. (2009) *Children's Rights in Scotland*, Edinburgh: W. Green

Martin, W. E. (2016) *Towards Compliance with CRPD Art.12 in Capacity/Incapacity Legislation across the UK: An Essex Autonomy Project Report Paper*, Essex: University of Essex

Mégret, F. (2008) 'The disabilities convention: Human rights of persons with disabilities or disability rights?', *Human Rights Quarterly*, Vol. 30, No. 2, pp. 494–516

Mégret, F. (2011) 'The human rights of older persons: A growing challenge', *Human Rights Law Review*, Vol. 11, No. 1, pp. 37–66

Meltzer, H., Lader, D., Corbin, T., Goodman, R. and Ford, T. (2004) *The Mental Health of Young People Looked After by Local Authorities in Scotland*, London: The Stationery Office

Miller, A. (2000) *Human Rights: A Modern Agenda*, Edinburgh: T. & T. Clark

Miller, A. (2016) 'Human rights need to come of age – the age of implementation', *Scottish Human Rights Journal*, pp. 1–2

Miller, J. M. (2010) 'International human rights and the elderly', *Marquette Elder's Advisor*, Vol. 11: No. 2, Article 6, p. 343

Morris, J. (1991) *Pride Against Prejudice: A Personal Politics of Disability*, The Women's Press

Morris, J. (2001) 'Impairment and disability: Constructing an ethics of care that protects human rights', *Hypatia*, Vol. 16, No. 4, pp. 1–16

Morris, J. (2013) 'Personal and political: A feminist perspective on researching physical disability', in Armstrong, F., Masterton, M. and Potts, P. (eds) (2013) *Equality and Diversity in Education 2: National and International Contexts for Practice and Research*, Abingdon: Routledge, p. 208

Mowbray, A. (2004) *The Development of Positive Obligations under the European Convention on Human Rights by the European Court of Human Rights*, Oxford: Hart Publishing

Mowbray, A. (2005) 'The creativity of the European Court of Human Rights', *Human Rights Law Review*, Vol. 5, No. 1, pp. 57–79

Mowbray, A. (2010) 'A study of the principles of fair balance in the jurisprudence of the European Court of Human Rights', *Human Rights Law Review*, Vol. 10, No. 2, pp. 289–317

Murdoch, J. (2008) *The Optional Protocol to the United Nations Convention for the Elimination of All Forms of Discrimination Against Women (CEDAW): The Experience of the United Kingdom*, London: Ministry of Justice

MWC (2010) *Consenting Adults? Guidance for Professionals and Carers When Considering Rights and Risks in Sexual Relationships Involving People with a Mental Disorder*, Edinburgh: Mental Welfare Commission for Scotland

MWC (2016a) *Response to Consultation on the Scottish Law Commission Report on Adults with Incapacity*, Edinburgh: Mental Welfare Commission for Scotland

MWC (2016b) *Statistical Monitoring, AWI Act Monitoring 2014/15*, Edinburgh: Mental Welfare Commission for Scotland

MWC and SHRC (2015) *Human Rights in Mental Health Care in Scotland*, Edinburgh: Scottish Human Rights Commission

Nirje, B. (1985) 'The basis and logic of the normalization principle', *Australia and New Zealand Journal of Developmental Disabilities*, Vol. 11, No. 2, pp. 65–8

NRS (2014a) *Household Projections for Scotland, 2012-based*, Edinburgh: National Records of Scotland

NRS (2014b) *Life Expectancy for Administrative Areas within Scotland 2010–2012 Including Revised Estimates for 2000–2002 to 2008–2010*, Edinburgh: National Records of Scotland

Oliver, M. (1990) 'The individual and social models of disability' (online). Available from URL: http://disability-studies.leeds.ac.uk/files/library/Oliver-in-soc-dis.pdf (accessed 12 March 2018)

ONS (2012) *Population Ageing in the United Kingdom, Its Constituent Countries and the European Union*, London: Office for National Statistics

ONS (2015) *National Population Projections for the UK, 2014-Based*, London: Office for National Statistics

ONS (2016a) *Estimates of the Very Old, 2002–2015*, London: Office for National Statistics

ONS (2016b) *Labour Force Survey*, London: Office for National Statistics

ONS (2017) *Mid-2016 Population Estimates UK*, London: Office for National Statistics

Orend, B. (2002) *Human Rights: Concepts and Context*, Calgary, Alberta: Broadview Press

Patrick, H. S. (2009) *Adult Protection and the Law in Scotland*, West Sussex: Bloomsbury Professional

Patterson, V. (1990) 'Whose rights?' A critique of the "givens" ', *Human Rights Discourse, Alternatives XV*, Vol. 19, p. 305

Rainey, B., Wicks, E. and Ovey, C. (2014). *The European Convention on Human Rights*, Oxford: Oxford University Press

Raymont, V., Buchanan, A., David, A. S., Hayward, P., Wessely, S. and Hotopf, M. (2007) 'The inter-rater reliability of mental capacity assessments', *International Journal of Law and Psychiatry*, Vol. 30, No. 2, pp. 112–17

Reed in Partnership (2011) *From Care to Independence: Improving Employment Outcomes for Care Leavers*, London: Reed in Partnership

Reed, R. J. and Murdoch, J. (2001) *Human Rights Law in Scotland*, London: Bloomsbury Publishing

Reed, R. and Murdoch, J. (2008) *A Guide to Human Rights Law in Scotland* (2nd edn), Edinburgh: Tottel Publishing

Reid, J. (1972) 'Alienation' (online), Rectorial Address Glasgow University. Available from URL: www.gla.ac.uk/media/media_167194_en.pdf (accessed 16 February 2018)

Richardson, G. (2012) 'Mental disabilities and the law: From substitute to supported decision-making?', *Current Legal Problems*, Vol. 66, No. 1, pp. 333–54

Richardson, G. and Thorold, O. (1999) 'Law as a rights protector: Assessing the Mental Health Act 1983', in Eastman, N. and Peay, J. (1999) *Law Without Enforcement: Integrating Mental Health and Justice*, Oxford: Hart Publishing

Robson, M. (1997) *Realising Human Rights: The Romanes Lecture for 1997*, Oxford: London Press

Rodriguez-Pinzon, D. and Martin, C. (2003) 'The international human rights status of elderly persons', *American University International Law Review*, Vol. 18, pp. 915–1008

Rose, N. (1985) 'Unreasonable rights: Mental illness and the limits of the law', *Journal of Law and Society*, Vol. 12, p. 199

Schuler, M. (1992) *Freedom from Violence: Women's Strategies from around the World*, New York, NY: OEF International

Scope (2011) *Deteriorating Attitudes Towards Disabled People*, London: Scope

Scottish Executive (2000) *The Same as You? A Review of Services for People with Learning Disabilities*, Edinburgh: Scottish Executive

Scottish Government (2010) *Self Directed Support: A National Strategy for Scotland*, Edinburgh: Scottish Government

Scottish Government (2012) *The Same as You? 2000–2012: Consultation Report*, Edinburgh: Scottish Government

Scottish Government (2014a) *Financial Impacts of Welfare Reform on Disabled People in Scotland*, Edinburgh: Scottish Government

Scottish Government (2014b) *The Impact of Welfare Reform in Scotland – Tracking Study Year 1 Report*, Edinburgh: Scottish Government

Scottish Government (2014c) *National Child Protection Guidance*, Edinburgh: Scottish Government

Scottish Government (2015) *Education Outcomes for Scotland's Looked After Children 2013/14*, Edinburgh: Scottish Government

Scottish Government (2016a) *Equality, Poverty and Security*, Edinburgh: Scottish Government

Scottish Government (2016b) *National Performance Framework*, Edinburgh: Scottish Government. Available from URL: http://www.gov.scot/About/Performance/purposestratobjs (accessed 16 February 2018)

Scottish Government (2016c) *Scottish Health Survey*, Edinburgh: Scottish Government

Scottish Government (2017a) *Mental Health Strategy: 2017–2027*, Edinburgh: Scottish Government

Scottish Government (2017b) 'Children's Social Work Statistics Scotland 2015/16' (online). Available from URL: www.gov.scot/Publications/2017/03/6791/downloads (accessed 16 February 2018)

Shakespeare, T. (2013) *Disability Rights and Wrongs Revisited*, Abingdon: Routledge

SHRC (2008) *Strategic Plan 2008–2012*, Glasgow: Scottish Human Rights Commission

SHRC (2012) *Getting It Right? Human Rights in Scotland*, Edinburgh: Scottish Human Rights Commission

SHRC (2013) *Scotland's National Action Plan for Human Rights 2013–2017*, Edinburgh: Scottish Human Rights Commission

SHRC (2016a) *Human Rights Based Approach to the Mental Health Strategy*, Edinburgh: Scottish Human Rights Commission

SHRC (2016b) *Human Rights in Health and Social Care – Putting Rights into Practice. Case Studies from Scotland*, Edinburgh: Scottish Human Rights Commission

SHRC (2017) *Gender Equality – Violence Against Women and Employment*, Edinburgh: Scottish Human Rights Commission

Series, L. (2015) 'Legal capacity and participation in litigation: Recent developments in the European Court of Human Rights', in Quinn, G., Waddington, L. and Flynn, E. (2015) *European Yearbook of Disability Law*, Leiden: Martinus Nijhoff

Shakespeare, T. (2013) *Disability Rights and Wrongs Revisited*, Abingdon: Routledge

Simpson, A. W. (2004) *Human Rights and the End of Empire: Britain and the Genesis of the European Convention*, Oxford: Oxford University Press

Skegg, A. (2005), 'Human rights and social work', *International Social Work*, Vol. 48, No. 5, pp. 667–72

Skills for Care (2013) *The Economic Value of the Adult Social Care Sector in England*, London: Skills for Care

Slavert, J. (2013) *Good Practice Guide: Deprivation of Liberty*, Edinburgh: Mental Welfare Commission

SPS (2016) *Prisoner's Survey 2015 – Young People in Custody*, Edinburgh: Scottish Prison Service

SSSC (2017) *Scottish Social Services Sector: Report on 2016 Workforce Data*, Dundee: Scottish Social Services Council

Stonewall (2011) *Lesbian, Gay and Bisexual People in Later Life*, London: Stonewall

Sutherland, E. E. and Cleland, A. (2009) 'Children's rights in Scotland: Where are we now?,' in Cleland, A. and Sutherland, E., *Children's Rights in Scotland*, Edinburgh: W. Green, pp. 1–22

Swain, J., French, S., Barnes, C. and Thomas, C. (eds) (2013) *Disabling Barriers: Enabling Environments*, London: Sage

The King's Fund (2014) *Background Paper: Attitudes to Health and Social Care, Review of Existing Research*, London: The King's Fund

Thomas, C. (1999) *Female Forms: Experiencing and Understanding Disability*, London: McGraw-Hill Education

Thomas, D. and Beasley, M. (1993), 'Domestic violence as a human rights issue', *Human Rights Quarterly*, Vol. 15, pp. 36–62

Together (2014) *State of Children's Rights in Scotland*, Edinburgh: Together (Scottish Alliance for Children's Rights)

Together (2016) *State of Children's Rights in Scotland*, Edinburgh: Together (Scottish Alliance for Children's Rights)

Treffert, D. A. (1987) *Dying with Your Rights On – Still*, 140th annual meeting of the American Psychiatric Association, Chicago: American Psychiatric Association

UN CESCR (1994) *General Comment No. 5: Persons with Disabilities*, Geneva: UN Committee on Economic, Social and Cultural Rights

UN CRPD (2009) *Guidelines on the Treaty-Specific Document To Be Submitted by States Parties under Article 35, Paragraph 1 of the UN Convention on the Rights of Persons with Disabilities*, Geneva: UN Committee on the Rights of Persons with Disabilities

UNDESA (2009) *World Population Prospects – The 2008 Revision (Highlights)*, Geneva: UN Department of Economic and Social Affairs

UN General Assembly (1993) *Vienna Declaration and Programme of Action*, Vienna: UN General Assembly

UN General Assembly (2009) *Follow-Up to the Second World Assembly on Ageing, Report of the Secretary General*, Geneva: United Nations

United Nations (1995) 'Report on the Fourth World Conference on Women: Beijing 4–15 September 1995' (online). Available from URL: www.un.org/womenwatch/daw/beijing/pdf/Beijing%20full%20report%20E.pdf (accessed 16 February 2018)

UPIAS (1975) *Fundamental Principles of Disability*, London: Union of the Physically Impaired Against Segregation

van Leeuwen, F. (2009) 'Women's rights are human rights: The practice of the United Nations Human Rights Committee and the Committee on Economic, Social and Cultural Rights', in Hellum, A. and Sinding Aasen, H. (2009) *Women's Human Rights: CEDAW in International, Regional and National Law*, Cambridge: Cambridge University Press, Chapter 8

Williams, J. (2004) 'Social work, liberty and the law', *British Journal of Social Work*, Vol. 34, No. 1, pp. 37–52

Williams, V., Boyle, G., Jepson, M., Swift, P., Williamson, T. and Heslop, P. (2012)

Making Best Interests Decisions: People and Processes, London: Mental Health Foundation

Wisdom in Practice (2014a) *Getting Older Feeling Valued – Older people in BME Communities Discussion Paper*, Glasgow: Outside the Box

Wisdom in Practice (2014b) *LGBT and Getting Older in Scotland Today: Discussion Paper*, Glasgow: Outside the Box

Wolfensberger, W. (2013) *The Limitations of the Law*, Ontario: Valor Press

Women and Work Commission (2009) *Shaping a Fairer Future*, London: Government Equalities Office

INDEX

A v. UK 36
accessibility problems 70, 76, 96, 106
accountability
    HRBA 45–6, 112
    Neary case 92
    Scottish Government 12, 13
    SHRC 14, 15, 16
    UNCRC 43, 47
    to young person 44
    see also PANEL principles;
      transparency
additional support needs xiv, 29, 70
Adult Support and Protection
    (Scotland) Act (2007) (ASP) 81,
    86–90
Adults with Incapacity (Scotland) Act
    (2000): *see* AWI
advocacy services 84, 85, 86, 99, 115
age factors 20, 99, 100, 101–3, 109
    see also children; older people
Age UK 108n36
Aintree University Hospital NHS
    Foundation Trust v. James 90
Alston, P. 7
Annan, K. 75
Anti-Social Behaviour Act (2003) 39
ASP (Adult Support and Protection
    (Scotland) Act (2007)) 81, 86–90
Audit Scotland 13, 18, 19, 67
austerity 19, 21, 23, 42, 64, 65, 67
Australia 80, 90
autonomy 71, 73, 77, 79, 82, 96, 108
    see also capacity concerns
AWI (Adults with Incapacity
    (Scotland) Act (2000)) 81–4, 87, 97

Bach, M. 72, 88
Barnes, C. 69
Bartlett, P. 80, 87, 91, 98
Bauer, J. A. 4
Bavacqua and S v. Bulgaria 60

Beasley, M. 52, 54
Beauchamp, T. 71
Bensaid v. United Kingdom 73
best interests approach 78, 83, 90
birth rates, in decline 101, 103
black and ethnic minorities (BME)
    102
Bogdanor, V. 8, 9
Bolt, R.: *A Man for All Seasons* 117
Bournewood case 85, 89
Brownlie, I. 7
Bunch, C. 52

Campaign for a Fair Society 87
Campbell and Cosans v. UK 36
Canada 80, 88, 96
Cantwell, N. 30
capacity concerns, legal/mental 68, 71,
    73–4, 75, 77, 78, 79–80, 81–4, 83, 87
care leavers 29
carers, unpaid 48–9
Carers UK 17–18, 51
Carver, R. 5
case law xiii
    children's rights 47
    disabled people 68
    ECHR 36
    ECtHR 36, 39, 60
    European 82
    older people 99–100
    social care 109–15
    UNCRC 34
C-Change Scotland 16–17
CEDAW (Convention on the
    Elimination of All Forms of
    Discrimination Against Women) 22,
    54, 56–8, 61–2, 104
CEDAW Committee 56–8
Centre for Women and Democracy 51
CESCR (Committee on Economic,
    Social and Cultural Rights) 93, 101

CH v. A Metropolitan Council 93–4
Charlesworth, H. 54
Charter of Rights for People with Dementia and their Carers, Scotland 114–15
Cheshire West v. Chester Council 88–9
Chetty, K. D. 21, 94
child abuse reporting 37
child custody 33–4, 44
child labour 32
child protection 28, 33–4, 37–8
Child Protection Case Conference 28
children 27–9
    demographics 27, 28
    in difficult circumstances 31–2
    dignity 42
    disabled 29, 30, 31
    equality 30
    lived experience 26
    marriage breakdown 33–4
    mental illness 29
    poverty 29
    privacy rights 38
    social care 27
    as soldiers 32
    see also children's rights; looked-after children
Children and Young People (Scotland) Act (2014) 40–1, 46, 47
Children's Commissioner 27, 41–2, 46
children's rights 25–7, 29–30, 34–5, 38, 46
Childress, J. 71
Chinkin, C. 54–5, 115
Christie Commission 13
citizenship xiii–xiv, 2, 14, 70, 74, 117
Cleland, A. 40
Coalition of Scottish Local Authorities (COSLA) 45
Coggon, J. 71
cognitive impairment 73
Commissioner for Children and Young People 26
Commissioner for Human Rights, Council of Europe 76
Committee on Economic, Social and Cultural Rights (CESCR) 93, 101

Committee on the Rights of Persons with Disabilities 77, 78–9
Committee on the Rights of the Child (CRC) 32–3, 42–3
common law 8
Community Care (Direct Payments) Act (1996) 70
Connolly, M. A. 21
Connors, J. 52–3
consent 55, 57, 74, 82–3, 85, 93–4
    see also capacity concerns; decision-making
Constitutional Reform and Governance Act (2010) 38n51
constructed decisions approach 83
Convention of the Rights of Residents in Care Homes for Adults and Older People 113
Convention on the Elimination of All Forms of Discrimination Against Women: *see* CEDAW
Cooper, Lord President 11
corporal punishment 36–7, 39–40, 42–3
COSLA (Coalition of Scottish Local Authorities) 45
Costello-Roberts v. UK 36
Cotterrell, R. 96
Council of Europe 7, 76
CR V. United Kingdom 108
Cracknell, R. 51
CRC (Committee on the Rights of the Child) 32–3, 42–3
Crenshaw, K. 49
Criminal Justice (Scotland) Act (2003) 37n45
criminal responsibility 30, 42–3, 47
Cross-Party Group on Alzheimer's 114–15
Crowther, N. 71
CRPD (United Nations Convention on the Rights of Persons with Disabilities) 75–80
    Article 3 75
    Article 4 76
    Article 12 77, 79–80, 81, 82–3, 88
    Article 16 66

Article 19 76–7
Article 23 93
General Comments 80, 81, 83
Optional Protocol 67, 75, 78–9
autonomy 77
equality 97
Hale 89
independent living 78
life enhancement 22
older people 104
PANEL principles 68
as participatory process 98
Scotland 78–9, 87
social model 30
transformative power 97
United Kingdom 78–9
cultural factors 47, 78

data-sharing 45–6
Dates-n-Mates 95
de Feyter, K. 1, 2, 3, 4, 7, 23, 118
De Wilde, Ooms and Versyp v. The Government of Belgium 74
decision-making
autonomy 71
empowerment 113
impaired 74
participation 16
substitute 82
supported 80, 88, 90
see also capacity concerns
Declaration on the Rights of the Child 29–30
defamation 37
degrading treatment 6n9, 33, 36, 55, 64, 108, 121
dementia sufferers 82, 114–15
dementia-friendly communities 113–14
demographics 100–1
ageing population 20, 101–3
children 27, 28
older people 115
women 50
deportation 33, 122
Deprivation of Liberty Safeguards (DOLS) 85, 88–90

see also liberty
derogation in time of emergency 5, 6, 126
Devolution Statute 11
Dhanda, A. 75, 119
Dicey, A. V. 8
dignity
children 42
citizenship 2
disabled people 76, 97
and equality xiii, 1, 52
ICESCR 4
non-discriminatory approach 64
older people 108
person-centred practice 43
SDS 20
SNAP 15
social care policy 23
UDHR 3
undermined 110
disability, medical/social models 30, 71–2
disability advocacy groups 85
Disability Discrimination Acts
(1995) 70
(2005) 70
disabled people
accessibility 70, 76, 96, 106
case law 68
children 29, 30, 31
citizens 70
dignity 76, 97
discrimination 66, 75
ECHR 73–5
ECtHR 74
equality for 70, 78, 96
housing 63–4
human rights 22, 66, 96
independent living 16, 69
private life 87
Scottish Government 50, 67–8
with social care 68
social exclusion 70
welfare reform 67–8
will and preferences of 64, 79, 83, 88, 92, 98
women 50, 51, 52, 64

see also CRPD
discrimination
  age factors 99, 109
  CEDAW 56
  disabled people 66, 75
  ECHR 63
  eliminating 62, 75–6, 93, 126
  gender-based 49
  intersectionality 49
  NHRIs 13
  SNAP 14
  women 65
Dodov v. Bulgaria 106
DOLS (Deprivation of Liberty
  Safeguards) 85, 88–90
  see also liberty
domestic law
  CEDAW 56
  ECHR 36, 40, 110
  gender-biased 54
  HRA 5, 45
  human rights treaties 14
  and international law 4, 12
  justiciable rights 47
  monist/dualist approach 5, 38, 56
  older people 115
  UNCRC 38, 42, 47
domestic violence
  ECHR 22
  ECtHR 49, 59, 60
  housing 62–3
  Human Rights Act 54
  public/private spheres 55, 60–1
  statistics 52–3
  victim/perpetrator 52, 53, 59, 60–1
  violations of rights 52
Donnelly, J. 3
dowry killings 55
Drake, R. 72
Dupré, C. 108

Ealing Council 62–3
ECHR (European Convention on
  Human Rights) 1, 2, 5–7
  Articles and Protocols 5–7, 121–7
  Article 1 5–6, 59, 121
  Article 2 6, 60, 61, 106, 121

Article 3 6, 35, 36, 60, 61, 64, 73,
  121
Article 4 122
Article 5 73, 80, 82, 122–3
Article 6 6, 106, 123–4
Article 7 124
Article 8 6, 34–5, 36, 58–9, 60, 63,
  64, 73–4, 91, 93, 108, 111, 124
Article 9 124
Article 10 106–7, 125
Article 11 125
Article 12 78, 80, 125
Article 13 36, 59, 125–6
Article 14 35, 45, 61, 62–3, 126
Article 15 5, 126
Article 16 126
Article 17 126
Article 18 127
Article 33 6
Article 34 6
Article 35 6
case law 36
children's rights 34–5
cultural context 78
disabled people 73–5
discrimination 63
domestic law 36, 40, 110
domestic violence 22
HRA 108
jurisprudence 22, 83–4, 87, 98
as living instrument 7, 36, 59, 65,
  73, 87, 98, 111
PANEL principles 68
private life 58–9, 123
rights 6
Scotland 10, 80–96
societal values 117–18
United Kingdom 12, 61
women's rights 58–65
economic well-being 50–1
ECtHR (European Court of Human
  Rights) 6, 7
  case law 36, 39, 60
  child protection 37–8
  disability/capacity 74
  domestic violence 49, 59, 60
  jurisprudence 35, 49, 52, 59–62,

65, 81, 98, 106
  McDonald v. the United Kingdom
    110
  older people 106
  Osman v. United Kingdom 60
  and UNCRC 34, 35–8
education 27, 29, 35n37
effective remedy, right to 125–6
EHRC (Equality and Human Rights
  Commission) 13, 45, 57–8, 67, 118
Elsley, S. 29
empowerment 16, 17, 63–4, 94, 113
  see also PANEL principles
Endicott, O. 1
enduring powers of attorney 90
Engender 48, 50, 51–2
England and Wales 10n17, 80, 85,
  88–90
equality
  children 30
  CRPD 97
  de jure 58
  dignity xiii, 1, 52
  for disabled people 70, 78, 96
  gender differences 48, 55–6, 62
  non-discrimination 16, 17
  of opportunity 111
  SDS 20
  see also inequalities
Equality Act (2010) 29, 62, 70, 109
Equality and Human Rights
  Commission: *see* EHRC
Eremia and Others v. Moldova 61
ethnicity 28n14, 43
  see also BME
eugenics 73, 78
European Convention on Human
  Rights: *see* ECHR
European Court of Human Rights: *see*
  ECtHR
European Union Agency for
  Fundamental Rights (FRA) 52
Ewing, K. D. 11

fair trial, right to 6, 123–4
family law 27
family life, right to 35n34, 63, 94, 124

Fei v. Colombia 33
female genital mutilation 55
feminist theorists 54, 55, 72
feminization of ageing 103
Fennell, P. W. H. 80
Finch, V. 4, 128
Finkelstein, V. 69, 70, 71
Finland 37–8
food provision 4
forced labour 122
FRA (European Union Agency for
  Fundamental Rights) 52
France 5
Fredman, S. 51, 62, 119
freedom of assembly and association
  125
freedom of expression 125
freedom of thought, conscience and
  religion 124
Freeman, M. 2, 30

gender differences
  bias 62–3
  CEDAW 54
  discrimination 49
  domestic law 54
  domestic violence 52–3
  equality 48, 55–6, 62
  life chances 48
  life-expectancy 50, 102–3
  participation 51–2
  social justice 48
gender pay gap 51, 62
gender skills gap 51
gender-neutral approach 48
Geneva Conventions (1949) 32
Geneva Declaration 29
Germany 5
Getting It Right? (SHRC) 14
Glass, K. 96
Global Targets on Ageing 105
Goodale, M. A. 119
Gooding, P. 97
Goodley, D. 67
Goodman, R. 7
Goodwin-Gill, G. S. 7
Grant, J. P. 34

Grdinic, E. 55
guardianship 21, 82, 84, 96, 120
Gunter v. South-West Staffordshire PCT
  64

*HA, R (on the Application of) v. London
  Borough of Ealing* 62–3
Hale, Lady 89, 90, 110–11
harassment 8, 14, 57, 62, 67
Hare, I. 21
harm, risk of 86–7
Harris, J. 25
Harris, P. 69
health and social care 4, 17–19, 106,
  108–9
Health and Social Care Partnerships 13
Heinisch v. Germany 106–7
Hendrik Winata and Li v. Australia
  33–4
Hendriks v. The Netherlands 33
Heydon, J. 8
Higgs, P. 113
HL v. UK 85, 88–90
Hobbes, T. 2
Hogan, K. 72
Hollomotz, A. 94
homelessness 17, 100
Hope, Lord 10, 10n18
Hopkins, C. 55
House of Lords 100
housing 4, 62–4
HRA: *see* Human Rights Act
HRBA (human rights based approach)
  accountability 45–6, 112
  adoption of 21
  dementia sufferers 115
  kinship care 45–6
  learning disabled people 15
  older people 109
  PANEL principles 16, 23, 27, 49,
    63, 64, 65, 86, 98, 111, 112, 113,
    115–16, 118, 120
  person-centred approach 43–4
  practice example 95
  SHRC 14, 15–16, 95
  SNAP 15–16
  social care 118–19

UNCRC implementation 46–7
HRC (Human Rights Committee)
  33–4
human rights 3
  citizenship xiii–xiv, 2, 117
  disabled people 22, 66, 96
  historical development 4, 23, 53–5
  inalienability 1–2, 3
  as legal discipline 7
  United Kingdom 8–10
  universality xiii, 1, 73
  see also international human rights
Human Rights Act (HRA) (1998)
  8–9, 38–40, 61
  CH v. A Metropolitan Council 93–4
  domestic violence 54
  ECHR 108
  international agreements/domestic
    law 5, 45
human rights based approach: *see*
  HRBA
Human Rights Commitments, UK 128
Human Rights Committee (HRC)
  33–4
Human Rights Futures Project 39
human rights law xiii, 1, 8–10, 53–4,
  76, 79, 119
human rights treaties 3–4, 104
Hunt, P. 70

ICCPR (International Covenant on
  Civil and Political Rights) 3–4, 31,
  33–4, 104
ICESCR (International Covenant
  on Economic, Social and Cultural
  Rights) 3–4, 31, 101, 104
Ife, J. 2
IFS (Institute for Fiscal Studies) 50
ILO (International Labour
  Organisation) 32
incompatibility, declaration of 11
independent living 16, 69–71, 76, 78
Independent Living Fund 70
inequalities 14, 15, 58
Institute for Fiscal Studies (IFS) 50
institutional care 77, 107–8
  see also residential care homes

International Bill of Rights 4
International Covenant on Civil and
    Political Rights: see ICCPR
International Covenant on Economic,
    Social and Cultural Rights: see
    ICESCR
International Federation of Social
    Work 21
international human rights
    commitments 12–13, 129
    conventions 43
    development of 2–5, 14, 15
    law 2, 54
    legal framework 17
    UNCRC 30, 46
International Labour Organisation
    (ILO) 32
international law 4, 5, 12, 56
international older persons' advocacy
    organisations 115
International Plan on Ageing 104
intersectionality 22, 26, 49, 101
Ipsos MORI 18n28
Ishay, M. 2
isolation 70, 71, 76, 100
    see also social exclusion

Jackson, Judge 91
Jackson, P. 44
John, King of England 2n2
Johnson, D. 30
Johnstone, R. 53
Juppala v. Finland 37
jurisprudence xiii
    ECHR 22, 83–4, 87, 98
    ECtHR 35, 49, 52, 59, 60, 61, 62,
        65, 81, 98, 106
    gender 48
    lack of 27
    legal capacity 74
    public/private spheres 55
justifiable assault 36–7, 43

Kavanagh, A. 9
Keene, A. 83
Kennedy, D. 59
Kerzner, L. 72, 88

Khaliq, U. 80
Kilkelly, U. 35, 36
The King's Fund 18
kinship care 44–6, 47
Kong, C. 79
Kontrova v. Slovakia 60
K.U. v. Finland 37–8
Kumar, C. R. 13

Labour Party 118
Law Society of Scotland 67, 81
LCT (Life Changes Trust) 113–14
League of Nations 29
Learning Disability Alliance Scotland
    91
learning disabled people 90–6
    AWI 82, 83
    Bournewood case 85
    capacity concerns 68, 83
    community-based service 119–20
    consent 82–3
    Dates-n-Mates 95
    guardianship 21, 82
    HRBA 15
    MWC 82
legal identity 74
legality 16, 17, 100, 111, 113, 115, 120
    see also PANEL principles
lesbian, gay, bisexual and transgender
    (LGBT) population 102
lesbian, gay or bisexual (LGB) 50
A Letter to a Young Person (Jackson)
    44
Lewis, O. 79, 80, 97
LGA (Local Government Association)
    67
LGB (lesbian, gay or bisexual) 50
LGBT (lesbian, gay, bisexual and
    transgender) population 102
Liberty 39
liberty
    and autonomy 71
    deprivation of 82, 85, 88–90
    rights to 39, 122–3
life, right to 6, 31, 60, 106, 121
    see also family life; private life
Life Changes Trust (LCT) 113–14

life expectancy 50, 101, 102–3
life outcomes 29, 48
Llewellyn, A. 72
Lloyd, Lord 110
local authorities
   allocation of resources 109, 110
   health and social care 19
   kinship care 45
   powers/duties 12–13
   residential care homes 111, 112–13
Local Government Association (LGA)
   67
Locke, J. 2
London Borough of Hillingdon v. Steven
   Neary 91–3
looked-after children 28–9, 45

McCormick v. Lord Advocate 11
McDonald v. the United Kingdom
   109–11
McGroarty, J. 4, 128
Mackenzie, C. 71
McQuigg, R. 54, 55, 59
Madrid International Plan of Action on
   Ageing 105–6
Magna Carta 2
A Man for All Seasons (Bolt) 117
Mandela, N. 99
marginalised people 41–2
marriage 30, 93, 111, 125
marriage breakdown 33–4, 44
Marshall, J. 29
Marshall, K. 34
Martin, C. 105
Martin, W. E. 80
MCA (Mental Capacity Act) 85,
   89–90
Mégret, F. 21, 99, 100, 115
Meltzer, H. 29
Mental Capacity Act (MCA) (2005)
   85, 89–90
mental health 29, 46, 71, 75, 78, 79, 81
Mental Health (Care and Treatment)
   (Scotland) Act (2003) (MHA) 81,
   84–5
mental health services 42, 84
Mental Health Strategy: 2017–2027

(Scottish Government) 84, 85
Mental Welfare Commission for
   Scotland: *see* MWC
Mercer, G. 69
MHA (Mental Health (Care and
   Treatment) (Scotland) Act (2003))
   81, 84–5
Miller, A. 2, 8, 9, 10
Miller, J. M. 101
Miola, J. 71
More, T. 117
Morris, J. 67, 69, 71, 72, 97
Mowbray, A. 53, 54, 59
Ms Natalya Tcholatch v. Canada 34
Murdoch, J. 8, 9, 11, 57
MWC (Mental Welfare Commission
   for Scotland) 21, 82–3, 93, 95–6

National Care Standards 15
national human rights institutions
   (NHRIs) 13–17, 67
National Performance Framework
   12–13
National Records of Scotland (NRS)
   102, 103
natural law theorists 2
Nazi regime 73
Neary, S. 91–3
NGOs (non-governmental
   organisations) 32
NHRIs (national human rights
   institutions) 13–17, 67
NHS Boards 13, 19
Nirje, B. 66
non-discriminatory approach 16–17,
   31, 39, 44, 64–5, 94, 112
   see also PANEL principles
non-governmental organisations
   (NGOs) 32
Northern Ireland Human Rights
   Commission 13
NRS (National Records of Scotland)
   102, 103

Office for National Statistics (ONS)
   102
Office of the Public Guardian 84

older people 100, 101
  case law 99–100
  CRPD 104
  demographics 115
  dignity 108
  domestic law 115
  ECtHR 106
  Equality Act 109
  gender differences 102–3
  healthcare 106
  HRBA 109
  institutional care 107–8
  intersectionality 101
  living alone 102–3
  PANEL principles 100
  rights 22–3, 99–100, 104–9
  social care 101, 103
Oliver, M. 69, 71
ONS (Office for National Statistics) 102
oppression 49, 63, 70
Optional Protocols 3–4, 32, 57, 67
Opuz v. Turkey 61, 63
Orend, B. 1
Osman v. United Kingdom 60

PANEL principles 16–17, 22
  CRPD 68
  cultural change 47
  ECHR 68
  HRBA 23, 27, 49, 63, 64, 65, 86, 98, 111, 112, 113, 115–16, 118, 120
  'The keys to life' 95
  older people 100
  person-centred approach 64–5
  Steven Neary case 91–3
parents
  after marriage breakdown 33, 44
  children's rights 35, 46
  disabled children 31
  lone women 51
  UNCRC 26–7
Paris Principles 13
Parliamentary Assembly, Council of Europe 7
Parmentier, S. 23
participation

Children's Commissioner 41
  disabled people 70, 76
  equality 51
  gender differences 51–2
  kinship carers 45
  private law case 44
  Roshni 43
  UNCRC 31, 46
  see also PANEL principles
paternalistic attitudes 87, 96
Patrick, H. S. 86
Patterson, V. 54
People First 69
perpetrators/victims 52, 53, 59, 60–1
personal care packages 21
personality, right to 9, 25
person-centred approach 43–4, 64–5, 83, 94
political activity of aliens 126
poverty 2, 29, 42, 46
power/vulnerability paradox 100
prisoner voting rights 11
private life, right to 83
  children 38
  disabled people 87
  ECHR 58–9, 123
  and family life 94
  R (W) v. Commissioner of Police 39
  residential care home closure 112–13
  violated 110, 111
Proclamation on ageing 105
proportionality test 83, 110
Public Bodies (Joint Working) (Scotland) Act (2014) 13, 19
public/private spheres 54–5, 57–8, 60–1, 65, 76
punishment/law 124

R (on the Application of Bernard) v. Enfield LBC 63
R (on the Application of Cowl and others) v. Plymouth City Council 112–13
R (W) v. Commissioner of Police 39
R (Williamson) v. Secretary of State for Education 39–40
Rainey, B. 58–9, 72

Raymont, V. 83
Reed, R. 8, 9, 11
Reed in Partnership 28–9
Reid, J. 25
religion, right to 39–40
reproductive rights 56, 103
residential care homes 111, 112–13
Richardson, G. 78, 97–8
rights
    absolute/procedural/qualified 6
    first-/second-/third generation 4
    holders of 119
    justiciable 47
    legalism 98
    and risks 93
    violations 7, 15, 23, 33, 37, 45,
        57–8, 59, 77, 87, 110–11, 115
    see also HRBA
Robson, M. 3, 119
Rodger, Lord President 11
Rodriguez-Pinzon, D. 105
Roosevelt, E. xiii, 23–4, 120
Roper, W. 117
Rose, N. 98
Roshni 43, 47
Ross, Lord 10n17

SA (Scotland Acts) 8, 9–10, 11, 25, 40
SAFE Project 43
safeguarder 87
Salontaji-Drobnjak v. Serbia 74
The Same As You? (Scottish Executive)
    90–1, 93
sati 55
Schuler, M. 53
Scope 66, 67
Scotland Act (SA)
    (1998) 8, 9–10, 11, 25, 40
    (2012) 25
    (2016) 25
Scotland's National Dementia Strategy
    114–15
Scotland's Parliament, Scotland's Right
    9–10
Scots law 10, 36–7, 46
Scottish Alliance for Children's Rights
    25

Scottish Care 113
Scottish Constitutional Convention
    9–10
Scottish Credit and Qualifications
    Framework (SCQF) 29
Scottish Executive: The Same As You?
    90–1, 93
Scottish Government
    child poverty 29
    Child Protection Case Conference
        28
    and COSLA 45
    disabled people 50, 67–8
    and ECHR 10
    Mental Health Strategy: 2017–2027
        84, 85
    National Performance Framework
        12–13
    SDS 20
Scottish Human Rights Commission:
    see SHRC
Scottish National Action Plan for
    Human Rights (SNAP) 14–16, 113
Scottish Parliament 10–12, 15, 25–6,
    62, 114–15
Scottish Prison Service (SPS) 29
Scottish Social Services Council
    (SSSC) 18
SCQF (Scottish Credit and
    Qualifications Framework) 29
SDS (Self-Directed Support) 13, 15,
    18–19, 20–1, 68, 114–15
security, right to 122–3
Self-Directed Support: see SDS
Series, L. 74
sexual needs and rights 93
Sexual Offences Act (2003) 94
sexual partner violence 52
Shakespeare, T. 69, 70, 71
SHRC (Scottish Human Rights
    Commission) 13
    accountability 14, 15, 16
    AWI 84
    Commissioner for Children and
        Young People 26
    Getting It Right? 14
    HRBA 14, 15–16, 95

mental health strategy 84
  pay gap 51
  poverty 42
  victims of violence 52
Shtukaturov v. Russia 74
Simpson, A. W. 8
Skegg, A. 3, 21
Skills for Care 18
Slavert, J. 75
slavery 122
SNAP (Scottish National Action Plan
  for Human Rights) 14–16, 113
social care 6, 17–19
  case law and practice examples
    109–15
  children 27
  dignity 23
  disabled people 68
  ethics of 119
  expenditure 18, 20
  HRBA 118–19
  HRC 33–4
  living a good life 21
  older people 101, 103
  women 48–9, 63, 65
  see also health and social care; SDS
Social Care (Self-Directed Support)
  (Scotland) Act (2013) 13, 20–1,
  69n9, 70, 82–3
social exclusion 1, 14, 55, 65, 69, 70,
  117
social justice 2, 48
social security dependence 50–1
Social Services and Well-being (Wales)
  Act 105
Social Work (Scotland) Act (1968) 85
societal values 69, 117–18
socio-economic rights 53
sovereignty 11–12
SPS (Scottish Prison Service) 29
SSSC (Scottish Social Services
  Council) 18
Stanev v. Bulgaria 85
Stoljar, N. 71
Stonewall 102
support services 17, 18, 76–7, 109–11
Surjit Kaur v. Lord Advocate 10n17

*Surrey County Council v. CA, LA, MIG
  and MEG* 88
Sutherland, E. E. 34, 40
SW v. United Kingdom 108
Swain, J. 69

Thomas, C. 69
Thomas, D. 52, 54
Thorold, O. 97–8
Together 40, 41
torture 6, 35n35, 55, 121
transparency 45–6, 92, 112
  see also accountability
Treffert, D. A. 96
Tyrer v. UK 36

UDHR (Universal Declaration of
  Human Rights) 3, 4, 24, 52, 72, 104
UK Joint Committee for Human Rights
  41–2
UNCRC (United Nations Convention
  on the Rights of the Child) 22, 30–2,
  39–40, 46
  Article 1 31
  Article 2 30, 31
  Article 3 31
  Article 5 39
  Article 6 31
  Article 7 31
  Article 8 38, 39
  Article 9 39
  Article 12 31
  Article 14 39
  Article 19 31, 35, 36, 37
  Article 21 106
  Article 23 30, 106
  Article 25 106
  Article 32 32
  Article 37 36
  Article 41 31, 32
  Articles 12–15 31
  Articles 26–28 31
  Optional Protocol 32
  accountability 43, 47
  case law 34
  Commissioner for Children and
    Young People 26

CRC 42–3
    domestic law 38, 42, 47
    ECtHR 34, 35–8
    implementation by HRBA 46–7
    international human rights 30, 46
    monitoring and oversight 32–3
    parents' rights 26–7
    parties to 30
    Scotland Act 40
    Scots law 46
    Scottish Alliance for Children's
        Rights 25
UNDESA (United Nations
    Department of Economic and Social
    Affairs) 101
Unicef 32
Union of the Physically Impaired
    Against Segregation (UPIAS) 70
United Kingdom 5
    age factors 100, 102
    capacity concerns 80
    CEDAW 61–2
    children's rights 38
    as constitutional monarchy 8
    CRPD 78–9, 87
    dualist approach 5, 38, 56
    ECHR 12, 61
    HRA 61
    human rights 8–10
    Human Rights Commitments 128
    parliamentary sovereignty 11
United Nations 2, 48, 117
United Nations Committee on the
    Rights of Persons with Disabilities:
    see CRPD
United Nations Committee on the
    Rights of the Child: see CRC
United Nations Convention against
    Torture 55
United Nations Convention on the
    Rights of Persons with Disabilities:
    see CRPD
United Nations Convention on the
    Rights of the Child: see UNCRC
United Nations Department of
    Economic and Social Affairs
    (UNDESA) 101

United Nations General Assembly 14,
    100, 101, 102
    CEDAW 55–8
    Declaration on the Rights of the
        Child 29–30
    older people 99, 100
    Open-Ended Working Group on
        Ageing 106
    UDHR 3
United Nations Principles for Older
    Persons 105
United Nations Secretary General 75,
    100, 106
Universal Declaration of Human
    Rights: see UDHR
UPIAS (Union of the Physically
    Impaired Against Segregation) 70

van Leeuwen, F. 65
victimisation, targeted 14
victim/perpetrator 52, 53, 59, 60–1
Vienna Convention on the Law of
    Treaties 4–5, 38n52
Vienna Declaration 53
Vienna Plan 104–5
violations of rights
    CEDAW 57–8
    child protection 33, 37
    disabled people 77, 78, 87
    domestic abuse 52, 59, 60
    EHRC 126
    HRBA 15–16, 23
    kinship allowances 45
    legal discipline 7
    older people 107–8, 115
    private life 110, 111
violence against women 49, 52–3,
    57–8
    see also domestic violence; victim/
        perpetrator
vulnerability 100, 107–8

Ward, A. D. 83
welfare guardians: see guardianship
welfare reform 50, 67–8
Welsh government 105
will and preferences 64, 79, 83, 88,

92, 98
Williams, J. 4
Williams, V. 83
Winterwerp v. Netherlands 74
Wisdom in Practice 102
Wolfensberger, W. 118
women
    demographics 50
    disabled people 50, 51, 52, 64
    discrimination 65
    disempowerment 61
    lived experience 48–9
    social care 48–9, 63, 65
    welfare reform 50
    see also gender differences; women's
      rights

Women and Work Commission 51
women-only shortlists 58
women's rights 55–8
    ECHR 58–65
    historical development 53–5
    see also CEDAW
work, paid/unpaid 48–9, 51
World Assembly on Ageing 104
World Conference of Human Rights
    14

X and Y v. Croatia 74, 106

Z and Other v. UK 35